AICPA

FINANCIAL REPORT SURVEY
MAY 1995

Illustrations of Accounting for Certain Investments in Debt and Equity Securities

A Survey of the Application of FASB Statement No. 115

Leonard Lorensen, CPA

AMERICAN

INSTITUTE OF

CERTIFIED

PUBLIC

ACCOUNTANTS

Copyright © 1995 by
American Institute of Certified Public Accountants, Inc.,
New York, NY 10036-8775

1 2 3 4 5 6 7 8 9 0 IR 9 9 8 7 6 5

Library of Congress Cataloging-in-Publication Data

Lorensen, Leonard.
    Illustrations of accounting for certain investments in debt and
equity securities : a survey of the application of FASB statement
no. 115 / Leonard Lorensen.
       p. cm. — (Financial report survey)
       "March 1995."
       ISBN 0-87051-165-3
       1. Securities — United States — Accounting. 2. Financial
institutions — United States — Investments — Accounting. I. Title.
II. Series.
HF5681.F54L65 1995
657 — dc20   95-13038
                                                           CIP

PREFACE

This publication is part of a series produced by the Institute's staff through use of the Institute's National Automated Accounting Research System (NAARS). The purpose of the series is to provide interested readers with examples of the application of technical pronouncements. It is believed that those who are confronted with problems in the application of pronouncements can benefit from seeing how others apply them in practice.

It is the intention to publish periodically similar compilations of information of current interest dealing with aspects of financial reporting.

The examples presented were selected from over twenty thousand annual reports stored in the NAARS computer database.

This compilation presents only a limited number of examples and is not intended to encompass all aspects of the application of the pronouncements covered in this survey. Individuals with special application problems not illustrated in the survey may arrange for special computer searches of the NAARS data banks by contacting the Institute.

The views expressed are solely those of the staff.

Richard D. Walker
Director, Information Technology

TABLE OF CONTENTS

Page

CHAPTER I   SCOPE AND PURPOSE OF THE SURVEY   1

CHAPTER II   BANKS   3
National Commercial Banks   3
State Commercial Banks   14
Savings Institutions, Federally Chartered   22
Savings Institutions, State Chartered   33

CHAPTER III   FINANCIAL ENTERPRISES OTHER THAN BANKS   45
Personal or Business Credit Institutions   45
Finance Services   53
Life or Accident and Health Insurance Companies   60
Fire, Marine, or Casualty Insurance Companies   69

CHAPTER IV   NONFINANCIAL ENTERPRISES   79
No Trading Securities Owned   79
Trading Securities Owned   99

I

SCOPE AND PURPOSE OF THE SURVEY

This survey is intended primarily to help accountants and auditors apply Financial Accounting Standards Board (FASB) Statement of Financial Accounting Standards No. 115, *Accounting for Certain Investments in Debt and Equity Securities*, which was issued in May 1993. FASB Statement No. 115 establishes standards of financial accounting and reporting for investments in equity securities that have readily determinable fair values and for all investments in debt securities. The Statement requires enterprises to classify debt and equity securities into these three categories: held-to-maturity, available-for-sale, or trading. Investments in held-to-maturity debt securities are required to be stated at amortized cost. Investments in available-for-sale or trading debt or equity securities are required to be stated at fair value.

Accounting for debt and equity securities in conformity with FASB Statement No. 115 requires considerable judgment. An accountant or auditor who is confronted with problems in applying the Statement can benefit from learning how other accountants are applying it in practice. Accordingly, this publication presents excerpts from recently published financial statements of forty-two companies that illustrate the application of the Statement.

The AICPA National Automated Accounting Research System (NAARS) was used to compile the information. The examples presented in this survey were selected from companies in the 1993–94 annual report file.

This survey contains many more examples of information presented by enterprises that provide financial services than enterprises that do not provide such services. The reason is that financial enterprises own a larger variety of debt and equity securities than nonfinancial enterprises.

II

BANKS

Most enterprises that provide financial services are banks. Examples of accounting for investments in debt and equity securities in accordance with FASB Statement No. 115 by twelve enterprises that operate primarily in the field of banking are presented below. The information is classified according to which of these types of banks is the primary component of the reporting enterprise:

- National commercial banks
- State commercial banks
- Savings institutions, federally chartered
- Savings institutions, state chartered

NATIONAL COMMERCIAL BANKS

CONTINENTAL BANK CORPORATION, DECEMBER 31, 1993

Continental Bank Corporation and Subsidiaries
Consolidated Balance Sheet
December 31
($ in millions)

	1993	1992
Assets		

. . . .

Consolidated Balance Sheet (continued)
($ in millions)   1993   1992

	1993	1992
Securities held to maturity (fair value: $611 in 1993 and $511 in 1992)	607	507
Securities available for sale	920	—
Securities held for sale (fair value: $499 in 1992)	—	495
Total securities	1,527	1,002

. . . .

Stockholders' Equity

. . . .

	1993	1992
Net unrealized security gains, net of income tax effect	35	—

. . . .

Continental Bank Corporation and Subsidiaries
Consolidated Statement of Operations
Year Ended December 31
($ in millions, except common share data)

	1993	1992	1991
Fees, Trading, and Other Revenues			

. . . .

	1993	1992	1991
Trading revenues	102	30	73
Security gains (losses)	5	(2)	7
Revenues from equity investments	198	150	131

. . . .

Continental Bank Corporation and Subsidiaries
Consolidated Statement of Changes in Stockholders' Equity
Year Ended December 31
($ in millions)

	1993	1992	1991
Net unrealized security gains, net of income tax effect			
Balance at beginning of period	—	—	—
Net unrealized security gains	35	—	—
Balance at end of period	35	—	—

. . . .

Notes to Financial Statements

Note 2 — Summary of Significant Accounting Policies

. . . .

Effective December 31, 1993, Continental adopted SFAS No. 115, "Accounting for Certain Investments in Debt and Equity Securities." This standard establishes more stringent criteria for classifying investments as "held-to-maturity" and requires investments categorized as "available-for-sale" to be carried at fair value, with any net unrealized gains or losses reported in stockholders' equity, net of related taxes. Prior years have not been restated pursuant to SFAS No. 115. See Notes 4 and 5 for further information on debt securities and equity investments.

. . . .

Securities and Trading Account Assets. Debt securities are classified as securities held to maturity only if there is intent and ability to hold until maturity. These debt securities are carried at amortized cost.

Prior to the adoption of SFAS No. 115, certain debt securities that were held for indefinite periods of time were classified as securities held for sale and carried at the lower of cost or market value. After the adoption of SFAS No. 115, these securities are classified as securities available for sale and carried at fair value, with unrealized appreciation or depreciation recognized in "Net unrealized security gains, net of income tax effect," a component of stockholders' equity. This category includes certain securities that may be used as part of Continental's asset/liability management strategy and that may be sold in response to changes in interest rates, prepayments, or similar factors.

The gain or loss on the sale of debt securities is determined by using the specific identification method and is displayed as a separate line in the statement of operations. All debt securities are evaluated individually to determine if an "other-than-temporary" decline in value has occurred, with any such losses resulting in a direct write-down of the investment.

Assets, predominately debt securities, are classified as trading account assets when purchased with the intent to profit from short-term market-price movements. Debt securities are carried at fair value unless they are traded in an illiquid market, in which case they are carried at the lower of cost or market. Other assets classified as trading account assets are carried at the lower of cost or market. A gain or loss on a trading account asset sale is determined by using the average cost method. Realized and unrealized gains and losses are included in trading revenues.

Transfers of securities generally are not permitted between trading account assets, securities held to maturity, or securities available for sale.

Equity Investments. Securities held by Continental's equity-investment subsidiaries are carried at fair value, with appreciation or depreciation recognized in revenues from equity investments. The fair value of publicly traded securities is based on quoted market prices, discounted where appropriate. Fair values for non-publicly traded securities are determined by management's estimates based on quoted market prices of similar securities, prior earnings, comparable investments, liquidity, percentage ownership, original cost, and other evidence. Management's valuations are approved by the boards of directors of the respective equity-investment subsidiaries.

Prior to the adoption of SFAS No. 115, equity investments held by other subsidiaries were carried at the lower of cost or market. After adoption, investments held by these subsidiaries that have a readily determinable fair value are carried at such value, with unrealized appreciation or depreciation recognized in "Net unrealized security gains, net of income tax effect." All other equity investments are carried at cost. The carrying value of equity investments held by these subsidiaries is reduced by "other-than-temporary" declines in value.

. . . .

Note 4 — Securities

Effective December 31, 1993, Continental adopted SFAS No. 115. See Note 2 for further information on accounting for securities.

Securities Held to Maturity. Book values, gross unrealized gains, gross unrealized losses, and fair values of securities held to maturity are shown below:

December 31, 1993 ($ in millions)	Book Value	Gross Unrealized Gains
U.S. Treasury and federal agency securities	$ 558	$ 4
Other securities	49	—
Total securities held to maturity	$ 607	$ 4
December 31, 1992		
U.S. Treasury and federal agency securities	$ 317	$ 5
Other securities	190	1
Total securities held to maturity	$ 507	$ 6

December 31, 1993 ($ in millions)	Gross Unrealized Losses	Fair Value
U.S. Treasury and federal agency securities	$ —	$ 562
Other securities	—	49
Total securities held to maturity	$ —	$ 611
December 31, 1992		
U.S. Treasury and federal agency securities	$ —	$ 322
Other securities	2	189
Total securities held to maturity	$ 2	$ 511

The amortized cost of securities held to maturity that were sold in 1993, 1992, and 1991 was $23 million, $251 million, and $871 million, respectively. Gross realized gains and losses on securities held to maturity were immaterial in 1993. In 1992, gross realized gains were $1 million and gross realized losses were $3 million, and, in 1991, $9 million and $2 million, respectively. Tax-exempt interest revenue on securities held to maturity was immaterial in 1993 and $2 million in 1992 and 1991.

Book and fair values of securities held to maturity by maturity distribution are shown in the table below:

December 31, 1993 ($ in millions)	Book Value	Fair Value
Within 1 year	$ 379	$ 382
After 1 but within 5 years	55	55
After 5 but within 10 years	14	14
After 10 years	159	160
Total securities held to maturity	$ 607	$ 611

Securities Available for Sale. As a result of the adoption of SFAS No. 115 on December 31, 1993, Continental transferred securities amounting to $665 million from securities held for sale, $157 million from loans, and $98 million from trading account assets to securities available for sale.

Cost basis, gross unrealized gains, gross unrealized losses, and fair values of securities available for sale are shown below:

December 31, 1993 ($ in millions)	Cost Basis	Gross Unrealized Gains
U.S. Treasury and federal agency securities	$ 548	$ 3
Other securities	363	29
Total securities available for sale	$ 911	$ 32

December 31, 1993 ($ in millions)	Gross Unrealized Losses	Fair Value
U.S. Treasury and federal agency securities	$ 1	$ 550
Other securities	22	370
Total securities available for sale	$ 23	$ 920

Fair values of securities available for sale by maturity distribution are shown in the table below:

December 31, 1993 ($ in millions)	Fair Value
Within 1 year	$ 26
After 1 but within 5 years	144
After 5 but within 10 years	47
After 10 years	703
Total securities available for sale	$ 920

"Net unrealized security gains, net of income tax effect" includes net unrealized appreciation on securities available for sale and certain equity investments as discussed in Note 5. The amount attributable to securities available for sale was $6 million, net of related taxes of $3 million.

Securities Held for Sale. On December 31, 1992, Continental reclassified $495 million of securities held to maturity to securities held for sale. The write-down of these securities to the lower of cost or market resulted in a loss of $4 million, included in security losses on the consolidated statement of operations.

Book values, gross unrealized gains, and fair values of securities held for sale are shown below:

December 31, 1992 ($ in millions)	Book Value	Gross Unrealized Gains	Fair Value
U.S. Treasury and federal agency securities	$ 414	$ 4	$ 418
State, county, and municipal securities	34	—	34
Other securities	47	—	47
Total securities held for sale	$ 495	$ 4	$ 499

Gross realized gains on securities held for sale in 1993 amounted to $5 million.

Note 5 — Equity Investments

Equity-investment securities are held by equity-investment subsidiaries and other subsidiaries and are considered to be available for sale.

The proceeds from sales of equity investments were $196 million, $191 million, and $156 million for 1993, 1992, and 1991, respectively. Gross unrealized gains were $108 million, $28 million, and $40 million in 1993, 1992 and 1991, respectively.

7

The following table shows the composition of the equity-investment portfolio:

December 31 (*$ in millions*)	1993	1992
Held by equity-investment subsidiaries		
Publicly traded	$ 144	$ 92
Non-publicly traded	316	233
Held by other subsidiaries		
Carried at fair value	69	—
Carried at cost	150	179
Total equity investments	$ 679	$ 504

....The cost basis and gross unrealized gains of equity investments held by other subsidiaries and carried at fair value on December 31, 1993, were $24 million and $45 million, respectively.

"Net unrealized security gains, net of income tax effect" includes net appreciation on equity investments held by other subsidiaries and carried at fair value and securities available for sale, as discussed in Note 4. The amount attributable to equity investments held by other subsidiaries was $29 million, net of related taxes of $16 million. "Net unrealized security gains, net of income tax effect" does not include appreciation on investments held by Continental's equity-investment subsidiaries.

HIBERNIA CORPORATION, DECEMBER 31, 1993

Hibernia Corporation and Subsidiary
Consolidated Balance Sheets
December 31
($ in thousands)

	1993	1992
Assets		
. . . .		
Securities available for sale	394,640	492,719
Securities held to maturity (estimated fair values 1993 and 1992: $1,551,832 and $973,315)	1,526,231	956,923
. . . .		
Shareholders' equity		
. . . .		
Unrealized gain on securities available for sale	10,252	—
. . . .		

Hibernia Corporation and Subsidiary
Consolidated Statements of Changes in Shareholders' Equity
(in thousands, except per share data)

. . . .

8

	Unrealized Gain on Securities Available for Sale
. . . .	
Balances at December 31, 1992	—
Cumulative effect of change in accounting for securities available for sale	10,252
Balances at December 31, 1993	$ 10,252

Notes to Consolidated Financial Statements

Note 1. Summary of Significant Accounting Policies

Securities. At December 31, 1993, the Company adopted Statement of Financial Accounting Standards (SFAS) No. 115, "Accounting for Certain Investments in Debt and Equity Securities." SFAS No. 115 requires the classification of securities into one of three categories: Trading, Available for Sale, or Held to Maturity.

Management determines the appropriate classification of debt securities at the time of purchase and re-evaluates this classification periodically. Trading account securities are held for resale in anticipation of short-term market movements. Debt securities are classified as held to maturity when the Company has the positive intent and ability to hold the securities to maturity. Securities not classified as held to maturity or trading are classified available for sale.

Trading account securities are carried at market value and are included in short-term investments. Gains and losses, both realized and unrealized, are reflected in earnings. Held to maturity securities are stated at amortized cost. Available for sale securities are stated at fair value, with unrealized gains and losses, net of tax, reported in a separate component of shareholders' equity.

The amortized cost of debt securities classified as held to maturity or available for sale is adjusted for amortization of premiums and accretion of discounts to maturity or, in the case of mortgage-backed securities, over the estimated life of the security. Amortization, accretion and accruing interest are included in interest income on securities. Realized gains and losses, and declines in value judged to be other than temporary, are included in net securities gains. The cost of securities sold is determined based on the specific identification method.

Note 3. Securities

As discussed in Note 1, the Company adopted SFAS No. 115 effective December 31, 1993. Prior to December 31, 1993, the Company classified securities as held for sale securities (available for sale) and investment securities (held to maturity) based on criteria which did not differ significantly from that required by SFAS No. 115. Held for sale securities were recorded at the lower of cost or fair value. A summary of securities classified as available for sale and held to maturity is presented below.

Realized gains and losses from the sale of securities are summarized below:

	Year Ended December 31,		
(*$ in thousands*)	1993	1992	1991
Realized gains	$ —	$ 17,190	$22,428
Realized losses	—	—	(4,627)
Net realized gains	$ —	$ 17,190	$17,801

. . . .

Note 3. Securities (continued)

| *($ in thousands)* | December 31, 1993 | | | |
Type	Amortized Cost		Estimated Fair Value	
Available for sale:				
Mortgage-backed securities	$	384,388	$	394,640
Total available for sale	$	384,388	$	394,640
Held to maturity:				
U.S. treasuries	$	496,954	$	509,386
Mortgage-backed securities		1,021,300		1,034,468
Other		7,977		7,978
Total held to maturity	$	1,526,231	$	1,551,832

| *($ in thousands)* | December 31, 1993 | | | |
Type	Gross Unrealized Gains		Gross Unrealized Losses	
Available for sale:				
Mortgage-backed securities	$	10,252	$	—
Total available for sale	$	10,252	$	—
Held to maturity:				
U.S. treasuries	$	12,680	$	248
Mortgage-backed securities		16,493		3,325
Other		1		—
Total held to maturity	$	29,174	$	3,573

| *($ in thousands)* | December 31, 1992 | | | |
Type	Amortized Cost		Estimated Fair Value	
Available for sale:				
Mortgage-backed securities	$	492,719	$	502,818
Total available for sale	$	492,719	$	502,818
Held to maturity:				
U.S. treasuries	$	517,822	$	525,622
Mortgage-backed securities		433,319		441,910
Other		5,782		5,783
Total held to maturity	$	956,923	$	973,315

| *($ in thousands)* | December 31, 1992 | | | |
Type	Gross Unrealized Gains		Gross Unrealized Losses	
Available for sale:				
Mortgage-backed securities	$	10,099	$	—
Total available for sale	$	10,099	$	—
Held to maturity:				
U.S. treasuries	$	8,160	$	360
Mortgage-backed securities		8,786		195
Other		1		—
Total held to maturity	$	16,947	$	555

10

The carrying amount and estimated fair value by maturity of securities held to maturity are shown below:

($ in millions)	December 31, 1993	
	Book Value	Fair Value
Due in 1 year or less	$ 101.4	$ 102.0
Due after 1 year through 5 years	395.5	407.4
Due after 5 years through 10 years	13.8	14.4
Due after 10 years	1,015.5	1,028.0
Total held to maturity	$1,526.2	$1,551.8

Mortgage-backed securities are classified according to their contractual maturity without consideration of contractual repayments or projected prepayments. Securities available for sale at December 31, 1993, include mortgage-backed securities of $745,000 due after 1 year through 5 years, $51,906,000 due after 5 years through 10 years and $341,989,000 due after 10 years.

NATIONAL CITY CORPORATION, DECEMBER 31, 1993

Consolidated Statements of Income
(dollars in thousands except per share amounts)

	For the Calendar Year		
	1993	1992	1991
. . . .			
Noninterest Income			
. . . .			
Security gains	11,922	25,697	25,661
. . . .			

Consolidated Balance Sheets

	December 31,	
(dollars in thousands)	1993	1992
. . . .		
Assets		
. . . .		
Securities held to maturity (market value $1,824,855 and $2,442,196, respectively)	1,763,025	2,358,365
Securities available for sale (market value $3,181,599 in 1992)	3,403,201	3,140,174
Federal funds sold and security resale agreements	611,743	363,898
Trading account assets	150,296	13,044
. . . .		

Notes to Financial Statements

1. Accounting Policies

. . . .

Securities and Trading Account. As further discussed in Note 4, the Corporation adopted SFAS 115 "Accounting For Certain Investments in Debt and Equity Securities" on December 31, 1993. As required by SFAS 115, management determines the appropriate classification of debt securities at the time of purchase and re-evaluates such designation as of each balance sheet date.

Trading account assets are held for resale in anticipation of short-term market movements and are valued at fair value. Gains and losses, both realized and unrealized, are included in other income.

Debt securities are classified as held to maturity when the Corporation has the positive intent and ability to hold the securities to maturity. Securities held to maturity are carried at amortized cost.

Debt securities not classified as held to maturity or trading account and marketable equity securities not classified as trading are classified as available for sale. Securities available for sale are carried at fair value with unrealized gains and losses reported separately through retained earnings, net of tax.

4. Securities

On December 31, 1993, the Corporation adopted the requirements of SFAS 115. The most significant impact of the new accounting requirements is that unrealized holding gains and losses on securities classified as available for sale are recorded in stockholders' equity. Previously, these securities were recorded at the lower of amortized cost or market, with unrealized losses, if any, reported in earnings. The adoption did not have a material effect on the results of operations for the year ended December 31, 1993 and prior period financial statements have not been restated. In accordance with SFAS 115, stockholders' equity at December 31, 1993 was increased $35.0 million (net of $18.8 million in deferred income taxes) to reflect the net unrealized holding gains on securities classified as available for sale, previously carried at lower of amortized cost or market. Also at December 31, 1993, certain securities netting to $617 million (at cost) were reclassified between held to maturity and available for sale in contemplation of adopting SFAS 115.

The following is a summary of securities held to maturity and available for sale:

(in thousands)	Cost	Unrealized Gains	Unrealized Losses	Market Value
Held to maturity:				
U.S. Treas. and Fed. agency debentures	$ 205,411	$ 1,682	$ —	$ 207,093
Mortgage-backed securities	804,830	8,260	4,214	808,876
States and political subdivisions	604,916	58,770	3,735	659,951
Other	147,868	1,092	25	148,935
Total held to maturity	1,763,025	69,804	7,974	1,824,855
Available for sale:				
U.S. Treas. and Fed. agency debentures	1,094,907	24,699	3,771	1,115,835
Mortgage-backed securities	2,070,502	11,667	2,789	2,079,380
States and political subdivisions	31,973	854	—	32,827
Other	152,015	27,693	4,549	175,159
Total available for sale	3,349,397	64,913	11,109	3,403,201
Total securities	$5,112,422	$134,717	$19,083	$5,228,056

Table heading: December 31, 1993

(in thousands)	Cost	December 31, 1992 Unrealized Gains	Unrealized Losses	Market Value
Held to maturity:				
U.S. Treas. and Fed. agency debentures	$ 381,571	$ 4,297	$ —	$ 385,868
Mortgage-backed securities	822,143	10,122	2,638	829,627
States and political subdivisions	794,629	74,346	4,120	864,855
Other	360,022	6,446	4,622	361,846
Total held to maturity	2,358,365	95,211	11,380	2,442,196
Available for sale:				
U.S. Treas. and Fed. agency debentures	816,353	14,123	1,906	828,570
Mortgage-backed securities	2,241,266	24,211	6,317	2,259,160
Other	82,555	12,963	1,649	93,869
Total available for sale	3,140,174	51,297	9,872	3,181,599
Total securities	$5,498,539	$146,508	$21,252	$5,623,795

The market values of securities are based on quoted market prices, where available, and on quoted market prices of comparable instruments when specific quoted prices are not available.

The following table shows the carrying value and market value of securities at December 31, 1993, by maturity.

(in thousands)	Held to Maturity Cost	Market Value	Available for Sale Cost	Market Value
Due in 1 year or less	$ 668,611	$ 673,928	$ 149,012	$ 147,075
Due in 1 to 5 years	804,499	844,103	2,787,572	2,819,748
Due in 5 to 10 years	164,150	169,179	254,079	254,306
Due after 10 years	125,765	137,645	158,734	182,072
	$1,763,025	$1,824,855	$3,349,397	$3,403,201

Mortgage-backed securities and other securities which may have prepayment provisions are assigned to a maturity category based on estimated average lives.

In 1993, 1992 and 1991, gross gains of $16.3 million, $28.6 million, and $29.0 million and gross losses of $4.4 million, $2.9 million, and $3.3 million were realized, respectively. Proceeds from the sale of securities totaled $2,595 million, $1,254 million, and $1,891 million in 1993, 1992 and 1991, respectively.

. . . .

STATE COMMERCIAL BANKS

FIRST EASTERN CORPORATION, DECEMBER 31, 1993

First Eastern Corporation
Consolidated Balance Sheets
The Years Ended December 31
(dollars in thousands)

	1993	1992
Assets:		
. . . .		
Trading account securities	98	60
Investment securities (approximate fair value $175,354 at 12/31/93 and $369,402 at 12/31/92)	174,163	366,925
Mortgage-backed investment securities (approximate fair value $227,458 at 12/31/93 and $198,876 at 12/31/92)	227,848	190,542
Securities available for sale (approximate fair value $171,798 at 12/31/93)	171,558	—

. . . .

First Eastern Corporation
Notes to Consolidated Financial Statements
(dollars in thousands, unless otherwise noted, except per share data)

1. Summary of Significant Accounting Policies

. . . .

Securities. Investment and mortgage-backed investment securities are stated at cost, adjusted for amortization of premium and accretion of discount to expected maturity in a manner which approximates the interest method because management has both the ability and intent to hold these securities until maturity. Securities available for sale are carried at the lower of amortized cost or fair value. Gains and losses on sale of securities are identified on a specific cost basis.

During 1993, the Financial Accounting Standards Board (FASB) released Statement of Financial Accounting Standard No. 115, "Accounting for Certain Investments in Debt and Equity Securities" (SFAS No. 115). The Company adopted SFAS No. 115 on January 1, 1994. Initial adoption is required to be reflected on a prospective basis. Under SFAS No. 115, debt and marketable equity securities must be classified into three categories: trading, available for sale, or held to maturity. Trading securities are bought and held principally for the purpose of selling them in the near term. Held to maturity securities are those securities for which the Company has the ability and intent to hold the security until maturity. All other securities not included in trading or held to maturity are classified as available for sale. Trading securities are to be carried at fair value. Held to maturity securities are recorded at amortized cost, adjusted for the amortization or accretion of premiums and discounts. Unrealized holding gains or losses on trading securities are included in earnings.

Unrealized gains and losses, net of the related tax effect, on available for sale securities are excluded from earnings and reported as a separate component of stockholders' equity until realized. If the Company had adopted SFAS No. 115 on December 31, 1993, total assets and stockholders' equity would increase by approximately $150.

14

5. Securities

The book value and approximate fair value of securities are as follows:

Investment and mortgage-backed investment securities:	December 31, 1993			
	Book Value	Gross Unrealized Gains	(Losses)	Approximate Fair Value
U.S. Treasury securities and obligations of U.S. government corporations and agencies	$159,018	803	(21)	159,800
Obligations of state and political subdivisions	250	8	—	258
Debt securities issued by foreign governments	1,508	22	—	1,530
Corporate stock	3,860	—	—	3,860
Mortgage-backed securities	227,848	203	(593)	227,458
Other debt securities	9,527	379	—	9,906
Total	$402,011	1,415	(614)	402,812

Securities available for sale:	December 31, 1993			
	Book Value	Gross Unrealized Gains	(Losses)	Approximate Fair Value
U.S. Treasury securities and obligations of U.S. government corporations and agencies	$169,470	28	(1)	169,497
Corporate stock	13	—	—	13
Other debt securities	2,075	213	—	2,288
Total	$171,558	241	(1)	171,798

Investment and mortgage-backed investment securities:	December 31, 1992			
	Book Value	Gross Unrealized Gains	(Losses)	Approximate Fair Value
U.S. Treasury securities and obligations of U.S. government corporations and agencies	$318,719	855	(11)	319,563
Obligations of state and political subdivisions	250	—	(1)	249
Debt securities issued by foreign governments	505	—	—	505
Corporate stock	3,470	—	—	3,470
Mortgage-backed securities	190,542	8,334	—	198,876
Other debt securities	43,981	1,703	(69)	45,615
Total	$557,467	10,892	(81)	568,278

Securities with a book value of $151,402 and $145,649 at December 31, 1993 and 1992, respectively, were pledged to secure trust funds, public deposits and for other purposes as required by law. The book value and approximate fair value of securities at December 31, 1993, by contractual maturity, are shown below. Expected maturities will differ from contractual maturities because borrowers may have the right to call or prepay obligations with or without call or prepayment penalties.

| | December 31, 1993 | | | |
| | Held to Maturity | | Available for Sale | |
	Book Value	Fair Value	Book Value	Fair Value
Due in one year or less	$ 35,837	35,984	169,470	169,497
Due after one year through five years	133,858	134,892	2,075	2,288
Due after five years through ten years	600	610	—	—
Due after ten years	8	8	—	—
Sub-total	170,303	171,494	171,545	171,785
Mortgage-backed securities	227,848	227,458	—	—
Corporate Stock	3,860	3,860	13	13
Total	$402,011	402,812	171,558	171,798

The components of securities gains and losses are as follows:

| | Year Ended December 31, | | |
	1993	1992	1991
Gross securities gains	$9,212	7,490	99
Gross securities losses	(31)	(487)	(204)
Securities gains (losses)	$9,181	7,003	(105)

FIRST HAWAIIAN INC., DECEMBER 31, 1993

First Hawaiian Inc., and Subsidiaries
Consolidated Balance Sheets
The Years Ended December 31
(in thousands, except shares and per share data)

	1993	1992

. . . .

Assets

. . . .

	1993	1992
Investment securities:		
Held-to-maturity (fair value of $1,144,327 in 1993 and $977,822 in 1992) (note 2)	1,132,025	951,189
Available-for-sale (note 2)	98,453	—

. . . .

First Hawaiian, Inc. and Subsidiaries
Consolidated Statements of Income
The Year Ended December 31
(in thousands, except shares and per share data)

	1993	1992	1991

. . . .

Other operating income

. . . .

	1993	1992	1991
Securities gains, net (note 2)	1,955	161	262

. . . .

First Hawaiian, Inc. and Subsidiaries
Notes to Financial Statements

Summary of Significant Accounting Policies

. . . .

Investment Securities. Investment securities consist principally of debt instruments issued by the U.S. Treasury and other U.S. Government agencies and corporations, state and local government units and asset-backed securities.

As of December 31, 1993, the Company adopted Statement of Financial Accounting Standards ("SFAS") No. 115, "Accounting for Certain Investments in Debt and Equity Securities." In accordance with SFAS No. 115, investment securities are classified in three categories and accounted for as follows: (1) held-to-maturity securities are debt securities, which the Company has the positive intent and ability to hold to maturity, and are reported at amortized cost; (2) trading securities are debt securities that are bought and held principally for the purpose of selling them in the near term and are reported at fair value, with unrealized gains and losses included in current earnings; and (3) available-for-sale securities are debt securities not classified as either held-to-maturity securities or trading securities and are reported at fair value, with unrealized gains and losses excluded from current earnings and reported in a separate component of stockholders' equity.

Certain securities which could be liquidated prior to their respective maturities under certain circumstances have been classified as available-for-sale. Unrealized gains or losses are reflected as changes to the capital account.

Prior to December 31, 1993, since the Company had both the ability and the intent to hold the investment securities to maturity, they were carried at cost, adjusted for amortization of premiums and accretion of discounts.

Gains and losses realized on the sales of investment securities are determined using the specific identification method.

. . . .

2. Investment Securities

As of December 31, 1993, the Company adopted SFAS No. 115, "Accounting for Certain Investments in Debt and Equity Securities." The adoption of this accounting policy had no material effect on the consolidated financial statements of the Company.

Held-to-Maturity. Comparative book and fair values of held-to-maturity investment securities at December 31, 1993 and 1992 were as follows:

(*in thousands*)	1993			
	Book Value	Unrealized Gains	Unrealized Losses	Fair Value
U.S. Treasury and other U.S. Government agencies and corporations	$ 914,868	$ 1,490	$1,321	$ 915,037
States and political subdivisions	177,876	12,530	413	189,993
Other	39,281	16	—	39,297
Total held-to-maturity investment securities	$1,132,025	$14,036	$1,734	$1,144,327

17

2. Investment Securities (continued)

(*in thousands*)	1992			
	Book Value	Unrealized Gains	Unrealized Losses	Fair Value
U.S. Treasury and other U.S. Government agencies and corporations	$684,734	$ 9,338	$265	$693,807
States and political subdivisions	196,270	15,346	25	211,591
Other	70,185	2,600	361	77,424
Total held-to-maturity investment securities	$951,189	$27,284	$651	$977,822

The book and fair values of held-to-maturity investment securities at December 31, 1993, by contractual maturity, excluding securities which have no stated maturity, were as follows:

(*in thousands*)	Book Value	Fair Value
Due within one year	$ 360,464	$ 361,485
Due after one but within five years	507,098	519,178
Due after five but within ten years	86,213	86,145
Due after ten years	143,920	143,188
Total held-to-maturity investment securities	$1,097,695	$1,109,996

Available-for-Sale. At December 31, 1993, the unamortized cost, which approximates fair value, of available-for-sale investment securities, by contractual maturity, excluding securities which have no stated maturity, was as follows:

	U.S. Treasury and Other U.S. Government Agencies and Corporations	States and Political Sub-divisions	Other	Total
Due within one year	$ —	$ —	$ —	$ —
Due after one but within five years	—	—	10,460	10,460
Due after five but within ten years	—	3,000	17,211	20,211
Due after ten years	3,202	22,700	41,880	67,782
Total available-for-sale investment securities	$ 3,202	$25,700	$69,551	$98,453

The Company sold certain trading securities and recognized a gain of $1,873,000 in the second quarter of 1993. The Company held no trading securities as of December 31, 1993.

. . . .

Gross gains of $2,038,000, $283,000 and $315,000 and gross losses of $83,000, $122,000 and $53,000 were realized on sales of investment securities during 1993, 1992 and 1991, respectively.

TRANS FINANCIAL BANCORP INC., DECEMBER 31, 1993

Consolidated Balance Sheets
December 31,
(*in thousands, except share data*)

18

	1993	1992
Assets		
. . . .		
Securities available for sale (amortized cost of $194,310 in 1993 and market value of $34,354 in 1992) (note 5)	194,736	33,539
Securities held to maturity (market value of $55,635 and $226,241, respectively) (note 5)	54,286	223,599
. . . .		
Shareholders' equity:		
. . . .		
Unrealized net gain on securities available for sale, net of tax (note 5)	255	—
Unrealized loss on marketable equity securities	—	(163)

. . . .

Consolidated Statements of Income
Year Ended December 31

(in thousands, except per share data)	1993	1992	1991
. . . .			
Non-interest income			
. . . .			
Gains on sales of securities, net (note 5)	1,034	873	202

. . . .

Notes to Consolidated Financial Statements

(1) Summary of Significant Accounting Policies

. . . .

Securities. Effective December 31, 1993, the company adopted Statement of Financial Accounting Standards No. 115, Accounting for Certain Investments in Debt and Equity Securities. Accordingly, all debt securities in which the company does not have the ability or management does not have the positive intent to hold to maturity are classified as securities available for sale and are carried at market value. All equity securities are classified as available for sale at December 31, 1993. Unrealized gains and losses on securities available for sale are reported as a separate component of shareholders' equity (net of income taxes) beginning December 31, 1993. Securities classified as available for sale prior to December 31, 1993, are reported at the lower of aggregate cost or market value. Securities classified as held to maturity are carried at amortized cost. The company has no securities classified as trading securities.

Amortization of premiums and accretion of discounts are recorded by a method which approximates a level yield and which, in the case of mortgage-backed securities, considers prepayment risk. The specific identification method is used to determine the cost of securities sold.

. . . .

(5) Securities

Effective December 31, 1993, the company adopted Statement of Financial Accounting Standards No. 115, Accounting for Certain Investments in Debt and Equity Securities. Accordingly, all debt securities in which the company does not have the ability or management does not have the positive intent to hold to maturity are classified as securities available for sale and are carried at market value. All equity securities are classified as available for sale at December 31, 1993. In conjunction with the adoption of Statement 115, $153.4 million of investment securities were transferred to securities available for sale. Unrealized gains and losses on securities available for sale are reported as a separate component of shareholders' equity (net of tax) beginning December 31, 1993. Securities available for sale at December 31, 1992, are carried at the lower of aggregate cost or market value.

The following summarizes securities available for sale at December 31, 1993 and 1992.

December 31, 1993 (*in thousands*)	Amortized Cost	Unrealized Gains	Losses	Market Value
U.S. Treasury and Federal agencies	$ 90,597	$ 358	$430	$ 90,525
Collateralized mortgage obligations and mortgage-backed securities	93,267	1,020	403	93,884
Equity securities	10,446	42	161	10,327
Total securities available for sale	$194,310	$1,420	$994	$194,736

December 31, 1992 (*in thousands*)	Amortized Cost	Unrealized Gains	Losses	Market Value
U.S. Treasury and Federal agencies	$ 33,539	$ 815	$ —	$34,354
Total securities available for sale	$ 33,539	$ 815	$ —	$34,354

The amortized cost and approximate market values of securities held to maturity as of December 31, 1993 and 1992, follow:

December 31, 1993 (*in thousands*)	Amortized Cost	Unrealized Gains	Losses	Market Value
U.S. Treasury and Federal agencies	$ 500	$ 1	$ —	$ 501
Collateralized mortgage obligations and mortgage-backed securities	32,848	817	49	33,616
State and municipal obligations	16,762	607	104	17,265
Corporate debt securities	4,176	79	2	4,253
Total securities held to maturity	$54,286	$1,504	$155	$55,635

December 31, 1992 (*in thousands*)	Amortized Cost	Unrealized Gains	Unrealized Losses	Market Value
U.S. Treasury and Federal agencies	$12,310	$ 38	$ 8	$ 12,340
Collateralized mortgage obligation and mortgage-backed securities	193,860	3,574	1,204	196,230
State and municipal obligations	5,439	304	92	5,651
Corporate debt securities	1,608	16	—	1,624
Other debt securities	399	13	—	412
Equity securities	9,983	1	—	9,984
Total securities held to maturity	$223,599	$3,946	$1,304	$226,241

Included in equity securities at December 31, 1993 are Federal Home Loan Bank and Federal Reserve Bank stock of $4,325,000 and $744,000, respectively. At December 31, 1992, these stock investments were $4,130,000 and $744,000, respectively.

The amortized cost and approximate market value of debt securities at December 31, 1993, by contractual maturity, are shown below. Expected maturities may differ from contractual maturities because borrowers may have the right to call or prepay obligations with or without call or prepayment penalties. Mortgage-backed obligations generally have contractual maturities in excess of ten years, but shorter expected maturities as a result of prepayments.

(*in thousands*)	Securities Held to Maturity	
	Amortized Cost	Market Value
Due in one year or less	$ 996	$ 997
Due in one year through five years	5,298	5,305
Due after five years through ten years	8,285	8,572
Due after ten years	6,859	7,145
	21,438	22,019
Collateralized mortgage obligation and mortgage-backed securities	32,848	33,616
	$54,286	$55,635

(*in thousands*)	Securities Available for Sale	
	Amortized Cost	Market Value
Due in one year or less	$ 7,092	$ 7,095
Due in one year through five years	50,728	50,611
Due after five years through ten years	32,777	32,819
Due after ten years	—	—
	90,597	90,525
Collateralized mortgage obligation and mortgage-backed securities	93,267	93,884
	$183,864	$184,409

Securities with a par value, which approximates carrying value, of approximately $110,229,000 and $94,671 at December 31, 1993 and 1992, respectively, were pledged to secure public funds, trust funds and for other purposes.

Gross gains of $1,054,000, $923,000, and $202,000 and gross losses of $20,000, $50,000 and $-0- were realized on sales of securities in 1993, 1992, and 1991, respectively.

BANCFLORIDA FINANCIAL CORPORATION, SEPTEMBER 30, 1993

BancFlorida Financial Corporation
Consolidated Balance Sheets
(in thousands)

	September 30,	
	1993	1992

Assets

. . . .

Trading securities — FNMA mortgage-backed securities	17,297	—
Assets available for sale:		
Securities (aggregate fair values of $296,589 and $275,724)	296,589	272,254

. . . .

Securities held to maturity (aggregate fair values of $220,312 and $199,306)	220,846	196,139

. . . .

Stockholders' equity:

. . . .

Unrealized loss on securities available for sale, net	(431)	—

. . . .

BancFlorida Financial Corporation
Consolidated Statements of Operations
Year Ended September 30
(dollars in thousands, except per share data)

	1993	1992	1991

. . . .

Other income:			
Unrealized gain on trading securities	668	—	—
Gain on sale of mortgage-backed securities	8,786	11,715	1,313

. . . .

Gain (loss) on sale of other securities	(9)	889	(392)

. . . .

BancFlorida Financial Corporation
Consolidated Statements of Stockholders' Equity
(in thousands)

	Unrealized Loss on Securities Available for Sale, Net
. . . .	
Balance, September 30, 1992	—
Change in unrealized loss on securities available for sale, net	(431)
Balance, September 30, 1993	$ (431)

. . . .

BancFlorida Financial Corporation
Notes to Consolidated Financial Statements

1. Summary of Significant Accounting Policies

. . . .

(b) Investments

Management determines the appropriate classification of its securities (equities, mortgage-backed and related securities, and mutual funds) and loans at the time of purchase or origination. At September 30, 1993, the Company adopted Statement of Financial Accounting Standards ("FAS") 115, "Accounting for Certain Investments in Debt and Equity Securities." FAS 115 requires the reporting of certain securities at fair value except for those securities which the Company has the positive intent and ability to hold to maturity.

Trading securities — Mortgage-backed securities that are originated by BancFlorida and held principally for the purpose of selling in the near future are classified as trading securities. These securities are recorded at fair value. Both unrealized gains and losses are included in the consolidated statements of operations.

Assets available for sale — Securities or loans to be held for indefinite periods of time and not intended to be held to maturity are classified as available for sale. Assets included in this category are those assets that management intends to use as part of its asset/liability management strategy and that may be sold in response to changes in interest rates, resultant prepayment risk and other factors related to interest rate and resultant prepayment risk changes. Securities available for sale are recorded at fair value. Both unrealized gains and losses on securities available for sale, net of taxes, are included as a separate component of stockholders' equity in the consolidated balance sheets until these gains or losses are realized. If a security has a decline in fair value that is other than temporary, then the security will be written down to its fair value by recording a loss in the consolidated statements of operations. Loans available for sale are recorded at the lower of amortized cost or fair value. Only unrealized losses are included in the consolidated statements of operations.

Securities held to maturity — Securities that management has the intent and the Company has the ability at the time of purchase or origination to hold until maturity are classified as securities held to maturity. Securities in this category are carried at amortized cost adjusted for accretion of discounts and amortization of premiums using the level yield method over the estimated life of the securities. If a security has a decline in fair value below its amortized cost that is other than temporary, then the security will be written down to its new cost basis by recording a loss in the consolidated statements of operations.

. . . .

2. Assets Available For Sale

Due to the implementation of FAS 115 at September 30, 1993, the Company's securities which are available for sale are recorded at fair value. Unrealized gains and losses on securities available for sale, net of taxes, are shown as a separate component of stockholders' equity on the consolidated balance sheets. At September 30, 1993, an unrealized loss of $431,000, net of taxes of $289,000, was shown as a reduction of stockholders' equity. Loans available for sale are recorded at the lower of amortized cost or fair value.

At September 30, 1992 all assets available for sale were recorded at the lower of amortized cost or fair value.

A summary of assets available for sale is as follows:

(*in thousands*)	September 30, 1993			
	Amortized Cost	Gross Unrealized Gains	Gross Unrealized Losses	Fair Value
Mutual funds	$ 2,039	$ 8	$ —	$ 2,047
Mortgage-backed securities:				
FHLMC	128,217	68	(405)	127,880
FNMA	167,045	194	(577)	166,662
Total mortgage-backed securities	295,262	262	(982)	294,542
Total securities	297,301	270	(982)	296,589

. . . .

	September 30, 1992			
	Amortized Cost	Gross Unrealized Gains	Gross Unrealized Losses	Fair Value
FAMC stock (a)	$ 41	$ —	$ —	$ 41
Mortgage-backed securities:				
FHLMC	116,964	1,199	(69)	118,094
FNMA	155,249	2,554	(214)	157,589
Total mortgage-backed securities	272,213	3,753	(283)	275,683
Total securities	272,254	3,753	(283)	275,724

. . . .

(a) Federal Agricultural Mortgage Corporation stock.

The amortized cost and fair value of mortgage-backed securities at September 30, 1993, by contractual principal maturity, are shown below. Actual maturities will differ from contractual maturities because borrowers have the right to prepay obligations without prepayment penalties.

(*in thousands*)

	Amortized Cost	Fair Value
Due after one year through five years	$ 24,005	$ 23,991
Due after five years through ten years	73,780	73,700
Due after ten years	197,477	196,851
	$295,262	$294,542

. . . .

3. Securities Held to Maturity

At September 30, 1993, the Company implemented FAS 115 which allows the Company to designate a portion of its securities portfolio as held to maturity. Due to this designation, sales out of this portfolio after September 30, 1993, are prohibited except under rare circumstances. All securities in held to maturity are recorded at amortized cost.

A summary of securities held to maturity is as follows:

(*in thousands*)

	September 30, 1993			
	Amortized Cost	Gross Unrealized Gains	Gross Unrealized Losses	Fair Value
Municipal securities	$ 277	$ 4	$ —	$ 281
Collateralized mortgage obligations	29,352	223	(27)	29,548
Mortgage-backed securities:				
FHLMC	75,898	—	(450)	75,448
FNMA	115,319	62	(346)	115,035
Total mortgage-backed securities	191,217	62	(796)	190,483
	$ 220,846	$ 289	$ (823)	$220,312

	September 30, 1992			
	Amortized Cost	Gross Unrealized Gains	Gross Unrealized Losses	Fair Value
Municipal securities	$ 149	$ 5	$ —	$ 154
Mortgage-backed securities:				
FHLMC	112,110	2,325	—	114,435
FNMA	83,880	837	—	84,717
Total mortgage-backed securities	195,990	3,162	—	199,152
	$ 196,139	$ 3,167	$ —	$199,305

The amortized cost and fair value of securities held to maturity at September 30, 1993, by contractual principal maturity, are shown below. Actual maturities will differ from contractual maturities because borrowers have the right to call or prepay obligations with or without call or prepayment penalties.

(*in thousands*)	Amortized Cost	Fair Value
Due in one year or less	$ 34	$ 34
Due after one year through five years	87	91
Due after five years through ten years	18,879	18,880
Due after ten years	201,846	201,307
	$220,846	$220,312

. . . .

PIONEER FINANCIAL CORPORATION, SEPTEMBER 30, 1993

Pioneer Financial Corporation and Subsidiaries
Consolidated Statements of Condition

	September 30,	
	1993	1992
Assets		

. . . .

Securities (Notes 1, 6, 7, and 11)		
Held to maturity (estimated market value of $488,000 — 1993 and $18,628,000 — 1992)	487,887	18,231,850
Available for sale (cost of $135,294,000 — 1993 and market value of $111,997,000 — 1992)	136,402,760	111,618,072

. . . .

Stockholders' Equity		
Net unrealized gain on securities available for sale (Note 1)	559,735	—

. . . .

Pioneer Financial Corporation and Subsidiaries
Consolidated Statements of Operations

	Year Ended September 30,		
	1993	1992	1991
Interest income			

. . . .

Securities			
Held to maturity	$4,590,321	$2,262,990	$5,987,002
Available for sale	6,542,595	6,825,554	6,459,016
Trading	36,087	21,824	1,229,175

. . . .

	Year Ended September 30		
	1993	1992	1991
Noninterest income			
Gain (loss) from securities (Note 1)			
Held to maturity	176,394	—	503,908
Available for sale	4,839,381	6,221,795	8,701,819
Trading	691,342	(349,115)	230,749

. . . .

Pioneer Financial Corporation and Subsidiaries
Consolidated Statements of Stockholders' Equity

. . . .

	Net Unrealized Gain on Securities Available for Sale

. . . .

Balance at September 30, 1992	—
Net unrealized gain on securities available for sale	559,735
Balance at September 30, 1993	$559,735

Summary of Accounting Policies

. . . .

Securities. In May 1993, the Financial Accounting Standards Board issued Statement of Financial Accounting Standards No. 115 (SFAS 115), "Accounting for Certain Investments in Debt and Equity Securities." SFAS 115 addresses the accounting and reporting for investments in equity securities that have readily determinable fair values and for all investments in debt securities. Investments in securities are to be classified as either held-to-maturity, trading, or available for sale. SFAS 115 is effective for fiscal years beginning after December 15, 1993, however, an enterprise may elect to initially apply the statement as of the end of an earlier fiscal year for which annual financial statements have not been previously issued. Management has elected to apply SFAS 115 as of September 30, 1993.

Investments in debt securities classified as held-to-maturity are stated at cost, adjusted for amortization of premiums and accretion of discounts using the level yield method. Management has a positive intent and ability to hold these securities to maturity and, accordingly, adjustments are not made for temporary declines in their market value below amortized cost. Investment in Federal Home Loan Bank stock is stated at cost.

Investments in debt and equity securities classified as available-for-sale are stated at market value with unrealized holding gains and losses excluded from earnings and reported as a net amount (net of tax effect) in a separate component of stockholders' equity until realized.

Investments in debt and equity securities classified as trading, forward commitments and open interest rate futures contracts not treated as hedges against net interest rate exposure are stated at market value. Unrealized holding gains and losses for trading securities, closed interest rate futures contracts not treated as hedges and forward commitments are included in the statement of operations.

Gains and losses on the sale of securities are determined using the specific identification method. Gains and losses on interest rate futures contracts treated as hedges against net interest rate exposure are deferred and accreted or amortized using the level yield method as an adjustment to interest income over the estimated remaining lives of the hedged assets.

. . . .

Notes to Consolidated Financial Statements

1. Securities

A summary of the amortized cost and estimated market values of securities is as follows:

September 30, 1993

	Amortized Cost	Gross Unrealized Gains	Gross Unrealized Losses	Estimated Market Value
Held to Maturity Corporate securities	$ 487,887	$ —	$ —	$ 487,887
	487,887	—	—	487,887
Available For Sale				
Mortgage-backed securities	79,022,098	492,371	946	79,513,523
Corporate securities	2,001,493	16,907	—	2,018,400
United States Treasury	50,657,639	176,736	—	50,834,375
Other securities	3,613,068	569,713	146,319	4,036,462
	135,294,298	1,255,727	147,265	136,402,760
	$135,782,185	$1,255,727	$147,265	$136,890,647

September 30, 1992

	Amortized Cost	Gross Unrealized Gains	Gross Unrealized Losses	Estimated Market Value
Held to Maturity				
Mortgage-backed securities	$17,576,627	$ 521,282	$262,367	$ 17,835,542
Other securities	655,223	137,565	—	792,788
	18,231,850	658,847	262,367	18,628,330
Available for Sale				
Mortgage-backed securities	1,912,211	167,273	—	2,079,484
Corporate securities	56,966,882	125,078	—	57,091,960
Collateralized mortgage obligations	47,077,607	327,586	—	47,405,193
United States Treasury	—	—	—	—
Other securities	5,661,372	450,423	691,431	5,420,364
	111,618,072	1,070,360	691,431	111,997,001
	$129,849,922	$1,729,207	$953,798	$130,625,331

The amortized cost and estimated market value of securities by contractual maturity are shown below. Expected maturities will differ from contractual maturities because borrowers may have the right to call or prepay obligations with or without call or prepayment penalties.

September 30,	1993		1992	
	Amortized Cost	Estimated Market Value	Amortized Cost	Estimated Market Value
Due in one year or less	$ —	$ —	$ 845,790	$ 1,007,345
Due after one year through five years	21,957,518	21,999,650	2,001,856	2,091,960

September 30,	1993		1992	
	Amortized Cost	Estimated Market Value	Amortized Cost	Estimated Market Value
Due after five years through ten years	31,189,501	31,341,012	54,965,025	55,000,000
Due after ten years	319,341	522,622	49,909,014	50,374,165
	53,466,360	53,863,284	107,721,685	108,473,470
Mortgage-backed securities	79,022,098	79,513,523	19,488,838	19,915,026
Marketable equity securities	3,293,727	3,513,840	2,639,399	2,236,835
	$135,782,185	$136,890,647	$129,849,922	$130,625,331

Proceeds from sales of securities available for sale were approximately $380,826,000, $404,365,000 and $505,750,000 during the years ended September 30, 1993, 1992, and 1991, respectively. Gross gains of approximately $6,142,000, $7,174,000 and $16,172,000 and gross losses of approximately $1,302,000, $952,000 and $7,470,000 were realized on those sales during the years ended September 30, 1993, 1992, and 1991, respectively.

. . . .

UNITED FINANCIAL CORPORATION OF SOUTH CAROLINA INC., MARCH 31, 1994

United Financial Corporation
Consolidated Balance Sheets

	March 31,	
	1994	1993
	(in thousands of dollars)	

. . . .

Investment and mortgage-backed securities:		
Available for sale — at fair value (amortized cost — $63,341)	62,086	—
Held to maturity — at amortized cost (fair value — $82,355)	83,795	—
Held for investment at amortized cost (fair value — $92,128)	—	89,977
Total investment and mortgage-backed securities	145,881	89,977

. . . .

Stockholder's equity:

. . . .

Unrealized loss in investment and mortgage-backed securities available for sale	(778)	—

. . . .

United Financial Corporation
Consolidated Statements of Income
(in thousands)

	Years Ended March 31,		
	1994	1993	1992
	(in thousands of dollars, except share and per share amounts)		

. . . .

Other income (expense):

. . . .

Gain on sale of:			
Investment securities	22	16	165
Mortgage-backed securities held for investment	206	17	98
Mortgage-backed securities held for sale	1,061	1,085	536

. . . .

United Financial Corporation
Consolidated Statements of Stockholders' Equity

	Unrealized Loss on Investments and Mortgage-Backed Securities Available for Sale
	(in thousands of dollars, except share and per share amounts)
Balance at March 31, 1993	—
Net unrealized loss on investments and mortgage-backed securities available for sale	$(778)
Balance at March 31, 1994	$(778)

United Financial Corporation
Notes to Consolidated Financial Statements

1. Summary of Significant Accounting Policies

. . . .

Securities — The Corporation adopted Statement of Financial Accounting Standards No. 115, Accounting for Certain Investments in Debt and Equity Securities (FASB 115), effective March 31, 1994. Under the Statement, debt securities that the Corporation has the positive intent and ability to hold to maturity are classified as "held-to-maturity" securities and reported at amortized cost. Debt and equity securities that are bought and held principally for the purpose of selling in the near term are classified as "trading" securities and reported at fair value, with unrealized gains and losses included in earnings. Debt and equity securities not classified as either held-to-maturity or trading securities are classified as "available-for-sale" securities and reported at fair value with unrealized gains and losses excluded from earnings and reported as a separate component of stockholders' equity. Transfer of securities between classifications will be accounted for at fair value. Concurrent with the adoption of the Statement, management reevaluated its intent with respect to its portfolio and, accordingly, reclassified certain investment and mortgage-backed securities to available-for-sale securities which resulted in a decrease in stockholders' equity of $778,000 (net of $477,000 deferred tax effects). No securities have been classified as trading securities.

Prior to adoption of FASB 115, securities were classified as held for investment when future events that could be reasonably foreseen, and would lead to a sale, were considered to be unlikely. Debt securities classified as held-for-sale and equity securities were recorded at the lower of aggregate cost or market value. Unrealized valuation losses for debt securities held for sale or recovery of previously recorded unrealized valuation losses were recorded in the statement of income in the period incurred. Unrealized valuation losses for equity securities, if any, were excluded from income and reported as adjustments to stockholders' equity. Transfers of securities between classifications were recorded at the lower of cost or market.

Premiums and discounts on debt securities are amortized or accreted as adjustments to income over the estimated life of the security using a method approximating the level yield method. Gain or loss on the sale of securities is based on the specific identification method. The fair value of securities is based on quoted market prices or dealer quotes. If a quoted market price is not available, fair value is estimated using quoted market prices for similar securities.

. . . .

2. Investments and Mortgage-Backed Securities

The Corporation adopted FASB 115, Accounting for Certain Investments in Debt and Equity Securities, at March 31, 1994 (see Note 1 — "Securities").

Available for Sale — The amortized cost, gross unrealized gains, gross unrealized losses and fair values of securities available for sale consisted of the following (*in thousands of dollars*):

March 31, 1994	Amortized Cost	Gross Unrealized Gains	Gross Unrealized Losses	Fair Value
Marketable equity securities	$13,325	$ 116	$ 97	$13,344
Mortgage-backed securities:				
FNMA Securities	4,697	—	319	4,378
Collateralized mortgage obligations	45,319	114	1,069	44,364
Total mortgage-backed securities	50,016	114	1,388	48,742
Total	$63,341	$ 230	$1,485	$62,086

Held to Maturity — The amortized cost, gross unrealized gains, gross unrealized losses and fair values of securities held to maturity consisted of the following (*in thousands of dollars*):

March 31, 1994	Amortized Cost	Gross Unrealized Gains	Gross Unrealized Losses	Fair Value
Investment securities:				
U.S. Treasury obligations	$ 3,036	$ 1	$ 15	$ 3,022
U.S. agency obligations	14,045	31	386	13,690
Corporate debt	3,854	186	—	4,040
Total investment securities	20,935	218	401	20,752
Mortgage-backed securities:				
FNMA securities	30,929	157	763	30,323
FHLMC securities	30,875	138	757	30,256

2. Investments and Mortgage-Backed Securities (continued)

March 31, 1994	Amortized Cost	Gross Unrealized Gains	Gross Unrealized Losses	Fair Value
GNMA securities	1,056	—	32	1,024
Total mortgage-backed securities	62,860	295	1,552	61,603
Total	$83,795	$513	$1,953	$82,355

Held for Investment — The amortized cost, gross unrealized gains, gross unrealized losses and fair values of securities held for investment consisted of the following (*in thousands of dollars*):

March 31, 1993	Amortized Cost	Gross Unrealized Gains	Gross Unrealized Losses	Fair Value
Investment securities:				
U.S. Treasury obligations	$ 4,053	$ 71	$ —	$ 4,124
U.S. agency obligations	5,992	107	—	6,099
Corporate debt	5,513	166	—	5,679
Marketable equity securities	11,157	195	—	11,352
Total investment securities	26,715	539	—	27,254
Mortgage-backed securities				
FNMA securities	24,017	732	—	24,749
FHLMC securities	17,065	559	4	17,620
GNMA securities	129	2	—	131
Collateralized mortgage obligations	22,051	323	—	22,374
Total mortgage-backed securities	63,262	1,616	4	64,874
Total	$89,977	$2,155	$ 4	$92,128

The amortized cost and fair value of securities at March 31, 1994, by contractual maturity, follow (*in thousands of dollars*):

	Available for Sale		Held to Maturity	
	Amortized Cost	Fair Value	Amortized Cost	Fair Value
Due in one year or less	$ —	$ —	$ 501	$ 502
Due after one year through five years	—	—	20,434	20,250
Marketable equity securities	13,325	13,344	—	—
Total investment securities	13,325	13,344	20,935	20,752
Mortgage-backed securities	50,016	48,742	62,860	61,603
Total	63,341	62,086	83,795	82,355

Expected maturities differ from contractual maturities; issuers may have the right to call or prepay obligations with or without prepayment penalties.

The mortgage-backed securities held at March 31, 1994, mature between 5 and 30 years. The actual lives of these securities may be shorter as a result of prepayments.

Proceeds from sales of investment securities for the years ended March 31, 1994, 1993, and 1992 were $5,117,000, $1,946,000 and $448,000, respectively, resulting in gains of $22,000, $16,000 and $165,000, respectively. No material losses were incurred. Such sales consisted solely of sales of marketable equity securities. There were no other sales of investments securities in fiscal 1994, 1993, and 1992.

Proceeds from sales of mortgage-backed securities held for long-term investment for the years ended March 31, 1994, 1993, and 1992, were $10,024,000, $2,645,000 and $2,858,000, respectively, resulting in gains of $206,000, $17,000 and $98,000, respectively. No material losses were incurred. All other mortgage-backed securities sold during such periods represented loans held for sale in connection with mortgage banking activities that were securitized prior to sale.

SAVINGS INSTITUTIONS, STATE CHARTERED

FAMILY BANCORP, DECEMBER 31, 1993

Family Bancorp and Subsidiaries
Consolidated Balance Sheets

	December 31,	
	1993	1992
	(in thousands)	
. . . .		
Investment securities (Note 3)	289,315	238,464
. . . .		
Stockholders' equity		
. . . .		
Net unrealized gain on securities available for sale, after tax effects	1,452	—
. . . .		

Family Bancorp and Subsidiaries
Consolidated Statements of Operations

	Years Ended December 31,		
	1993	1992	1991
	(in thousands, except per share data)		
. . . .			
Other income:			
. . . .			
Gain on securities, net	1,878	1,334	3,143
. . . .			

Family Bancorp and Subsidiaries
Consolidated Statements of Changes in Stockholders' Equity

	(*in thousands*) Net Unrealized Gain on Securities Available for Sale
Balance at December 31, 1992	—
Change in method of accounting for investment securities, after tax effects (Note 1)	<u>1,452</u>
Balance at December 31, 1993	$1,452

Family Bancorp and Subsidiaries
Notes to Consolidated Financial Statements
Years Ended December 31, 1993, 1992, and 1991

1. Summary of Significant Accounting Policies

. . . .

Accounting Policy Changes

Investment Securities. Effective December 31, 1993, the Company adopted the provisions of Financial Accounting Standards Board Statement of Financial Accounting Standards ("SFAS") No. 115, "Accounting for Certain Investments in Debt and Equity Securities." The Statement establishes standards for all debt securities and for equity securities that have readily determinable fair values. As required under SFAS No. 115, prior year financial statements have not been restated.

SFAS No. 115 requires that investments in debt securities that management has the positive intent and ability to hold to maturity be classified as "held to maturity" and reflected at amortized cost. Investments that are purchased and held principally for the purpose of selling them in the near term are classified as "trading securities" and reflected on the balance sheet at fair value, with unrealized gains and losses included in earnings. Investments not classified as either of the above are classified as "available for sale" and reflected on the balance sheet at fair value, with unrealized gains and losses excluded from earnings and reported as a separate component of stockholders' equity. The cumulative effect of the change in accounting principle at December 31, 1993, is to increase stockholders' equity by $1,452,000 net of related income tax effects. There was no effect on net income for the year ended December 31, 1993 relating to the adoption of SFAS No. 115.

Prior to December 31, 1993, debt securities that management had the intent and ability to hold until maturity were reflected at amortized cost. Marketable equity securities held for sale were stated at the lower of aggregate cost or fair value. Net unrealized losses applicable to marketable equity securities were reflected as a charge to stockholders' equity while write-downs applicable to securities held for sale were reflected in operations.

For all years presented, other equity securities are reflected at cost. Purchase premiums and discounts are amortized to earnings by a method which approximates the interest method over the terms of the investments. Declines in the value of investments that are deemed to be other than temporary are reflected in earnings when identified. Gains and losses on disposition of investments are computed by the specific identification method.

. . . .

3. Investment Securities

Investment securities consist of the following and reflect the change in accounting principle as disclosed in Note 1 to the consolidated financial statements:

	December 31, 1993	December 31, 1992
	(in thousands)	
Securities available for sale, at fair value	$196,423	$ —
Securities held to maturity, at amortized cost	87,905	—
Securities held for investment (debt securities at amortized cost; marketable equity securities at lower of cost or fair value)	—	233,492
Restricted equity securities:		
Federal Home Loan Bank of Boston	3,511	3,985
The Saving Bank Life Insurance Company of Massachusetts	1,476	987
	$289,315	$238,464

The amortized cost and estimated fair value of investment securities, with gross unrealized gains and losses, follow:

	December 31, 1993			
	Amortized Cost	Gross Unrealized Gains	Gross Unrealized Losses	Fair Value
	(in thousands)			
Securities Available for Sale				
Debt securities:				
U.S. Government	$ 19,513	$ 459	$ (4)	$ 19,968
Federal agency	11,020	152	(50)	11,122
Corporate	41,281	531	(106)	41,706
Mortgage-backed	72,220	657	(330)	72,547
REMICs and CMOs	35,586	194	(208)	35,554
Total debt securities	179,602	1,993	(698)	180,897
Marketable equity securities	14,400	1,246	(120)	15,526
Total securities available for sale	$194,002	$3,239	$(818)	$196,423
Securities Held to Maturity				
U.S. Government	$ 5,006	$ 58	$ —	$ 5,064
Federal agency	3,101	153	—	3,254
Corporate	24,826	989	(3)	25,812
Other	1,012	5	(3)	1,014
Mortgage-backed	45,778	1,309	(21)	47,066
REMICs and CMOs	6,678	159	—	6,837
Other asset-backed	1,504	85	—	1,589
Total securities held to maturity	$87,905	$2,758	$ (27)	$90,636

At December 31, 1993, the Company has pledged U.S. Government obligations with an amortized cost of $1,006,000, and a fair value of $1,039,000, as collateral against its treasury, tax and loan account.

At December 31, 1993, the Company owed $13,476,000 to brokers for securities that were purchased in December, 1993, but for which delivery and payment were not due until January, 1994.

The amortized cost and estimated fair value of debt securities by contractual maturity at December 31, 1993, are as follows:

| | Available for Sale | | Held to Maturity | |
	Amortized Cost	Fair Value	Amortized Cost	Fair Value
	(in thousands)			
Within 1 year	$ 7,158	$ 7,258	$14,149	$14,381
After 1 year through 5 years	55,061	55,921	17,566	18,513
After 5 years through 10 years	5,869	5,847	2,230	2,250
After 10 years through 20 years	2,731	2,762	—	—
After 20 years	995	1,008	—	—
	71,814	72,796	33,945	35,144
Asset-backed securities	107,788	108,101	53,960	55,492
	$179,602	$180,897	$87,905	$90,636

The amortized cost and estimated fair value of investment securities, with gross unrealized gains and losses, follow:

| | December 31, 1992 | | | |
	Amortized Cost	Gross Unrealized Gains	Gross Unrealized Losses	Fair Value
	(in thousands)			
Debt securities:				
U.S. Government	$ 22,522	$ 731	$ —	$ 23,253
Federal agency	11,323	191	(8)	11,506
Corporate and other	53,771	1,250	(439)	54,582
Mortgage-backed	102,959	2,580	(135)	105,404
REMICs and CMOs	38,112	510	(191)	38,431
Other asset-backed	2,547	98	—	2,645
Total debt securities	231,234	5,360	(773)	235,821
Less allowance for losses	(120)	—	120	—
Total debt securities, net	231,114	5,360	(653)	235,821
Marketable equity securities	2,378	617	(4)	2,991
Total securities held for investment	$233,492	$5,977	$(657)	$238,812

The amortized cost and estimated fair value of debt securities by contractual maturity at December 31, 1992, are as follow:

	Amortized Cost	Fair Value
	(in thousands)	
Within 1 year	$ 12,036	$ 12,288
After 1 year through 5 years	65,307	67,014
After 5 years through 10 years	3,565	3,560
After 10 years through 20 years	4,748	4,469
After 20 years	1,960	2,010
	87,616	89,341
Asset-backed securities	143,618	146,480
	$231,234	$235,821

Proceeds from the sale of debt securities during 1993, 1992 and 1991 were $72,104,000, $164,714,000, and $178,561,000, respectively. Gross gains of $1,866,000, $2,230,000, and $2,707,000 were realized during 1993, 1992 and 1991, respectively, and gross losses of $0, $423,000, and $173,000 were realized during 1993, 1992 and 1991, respectively.

DOWNEY SAVINGS & LOAN ASSOCIATION, DECEMBER 31, 1993

Downey Savings and Loan Association and Subsidiaries
Consolidated Balance Sheets
December 31, 1993 and 1992
(dollars in thousands)

	1993	1992
Assets		
. . . .		
U.S. Treasury and agency obligations and other investment securities being held to maturity, at amortized cost (estimated market value of $108,450 at December 31, 1993, and $98,937 at December 31, 1992) (Note 3)	105,265	95,248
Mortgage-backed securities purchased under resale agreements (Note 3)	110,000	270,000
. . . .		
Mortgage-backed securities held to maturity, at amortized cost (estimated market value of $53,143 at December 31, 1993, and $51,603 at December 31, 1992) (Notes 4 and 18)	51,060	49,339

. . . .

Downey Savings and Loan Association and Subsidiaries
Consolidated Statements of Income
For the Years Ended December 31, 1993, 1992, and 1991
(dollars in thousands)

	1993	1992	1991
. . . .			
Secondary marketing activities:			
. . . .			
Net gains (losses) on sales of loans, mortgage-backed securities and market valuation adjustments (Notes 4 and 5)	1,665	(2,588)	1,488
Net gains (losses) on sales of investment securities and market valuation adjustments (Note 3)	—	25	(14,725)

. . . .

Downey Savings and Loan Association and Subsidiaries
Notes to Consolidated Financial Statements
The Years Ended December 31, 1993, 1992, and 1991

(1) Summary of Significant Accounting Policies

. . . .

The Company is required to carry its available for sale or held for trading mortgage-backed securities portfolios, real estate acquired in settlement of loans, and real estate held for investment or under development at the lower of cost or fair value or in certain cases, at fair value. See further discussion under "Securities Purchased Under Resale Agreements, U.S. Treasury and Agency Obligations, Other Investment Securities and Mortgage-Backed Securities."

Securities Purchased Under Resale Agreements, U.S.Treasury and Agency Obligations, Other Investment Securities and Mortgage-Backed Securities. During 1993, the Company adopted Statement of Financial Accounting Standards No. 115 ("SFAS 115"), Accounting for Certain Investments in Debt and Equity Securities. SFAS 115 requires specific disclosures for debt securities and marketable equity securities (including mortgage-backed securities). Investments are required to be separately classified as "held to maturity," "available for sale" and "held for trading." Under the statement, securities classified as available for sale or held for trading must be carried at fair value, determined on an individual security basis, while securities deemed held to maturity will continue to be reported at amortized cost. Unrealized gains and losses for securities classified as available for sale are reported as a separate component of stockholders' equity. Unrealized gains and losses for trading securities are included in earnings.

The Company has established written guidelines and objectives for its investing activities. At the time of purchase of a security purchased under resale agreement, U.S. Treasury and agency obligation, other investment security or a mortgage-backed security, management of the Company designates the security as either held to maturity, available for sale or held for trading based on the Company's investment objectives, operational needs and intent. The Company then monitors its investment activities to assure that those activities are consistent with the established guidelines and objectives.

Held to Maturity. Securities held to maturity are carried at cost, adjusted for amortization of premiums and accretion of discounts which are recognized in interest income using the interest method. Mortgage-backed securities represent participating interests in pools of long-term first mortgage loans originated and serviced by the issuers of the securities. Mortgage-backed securities held to maturity are carried at unpaid principal balances, adjusted for unamortized premiums and unearned discounts. Premiums and discounts on mortgage-backed securities are amortized using the interest method over the remaining period to contractual maturity, adjusted for anticipated prepayments. It is the positive intent of the Company, and the Company has the ability, to hold these securities until maturity as part of its portfolio of long-term interest earning assets.

Available for Sale. Securities available for sale are carried at market value. Unrealized holding gains and losses, or valuation allowances established for net unrealized losses, shall be excluded from earnings and reported as a net amount in a separate component of stockholders' equity until realized.

Realized gains and losses on the sale of securities available for sale, determined using the specific identification method and recorded on a trade date basis, are reflected in earnings.

Held for Trading. Securities held for trading are carried at market value. Realized and unrealized gains and losses are reflected in earnings.

. . . .

(3) Mortgage-Backed Securities Purchased Under Resale Agreements, U.S. Treasury and Agency Obligations and Other Investment Securities Held to Maturity

Mortgage-Backed Securities Purchased Under Resale Agreements. Securities purchased under resale agreements amounted to $110,000,000 and $270,000,000 at December 31, 1993 and 1992, respectively. These agreements mature within one year and bear a weighted average interest rate of 3.71% and 3.89% at December 31, 1993 and 1992, respectively. Mortgage-backed securities collateralizing these agreements at December 31, 1993 and 1992 had a fair value of approximately $136,351,000 and $319,371,000, respectively, and were held in safekeeping on Downey's behalf of several major national brokerage firms and third-party custodians. The average interest rate and balance was 3.40% and $180,968,000, respectively, during 1993, compared to 3.99% and $282,400,000, respectively, during 1992. The maximum amount outstanding at any month-end during 1993 and 1992 was $210,000,000 and $395,000,000, respectively.

U.S. Treasury and Agency Obligations and Other Investment Securities. The amortized cost and estimated market value of U.S. Treasury and agency obligations and other investment securities held to maturity are summarized as follows:

	Amortized Cost	Gross Unrealized Gains	Gross Unrealized Losses	Estimated Market Value
		(in thousands)		
December 31, 1993	$105,265	$3,219	$ 34	$108,450
December 31, 1992	$ 95,248	$3,689	$ —	$ 98,937

The amortized cost and estimated market value of U.S. Treasury and agency obligations and other investment securities held to maturity at December 31, 1993, by contractual maturity, are shown below.

	Within 1 Year	After 1 Through 5 Years [1]	Total Amortized Cost
		(in thousands)	
U.S. Treasury and agency obligations:			
Amortized cost	$23,917	$81,348	$105,265
Estimated market value	$24,264	$84,186	$108,450

(1) No investment matures beyond five years.

In August 1991, in conjunction with an examination by the Office of Thrift Supervision, the Company reclassified its $252 million of long-term U.S. Government bonds from held for investment to held for trading. This change in classification required the Company to reflect these securities in its financial statements at fair market value rather than on a cost basis. This change in classification resulted in a loss of $13,730,000 during 1991. These securities were sold prior to December 31, 1991.

Proceeds, gross realized gains and losses on the sales of U.S. Government obligations and other investment securities are summarized as follows:

	1993	1992	1991
		(in thousands)	
Proceeds	$ —	$ 2,247	$385,150
Gross realized gains	$ —	$ 25	$ 1,495
Gross realized losses	$ —	$ —	$(19,810)

(4) Mortgage-Backed Securities Held to Maturity

The amortized cost and estimated market value of mortgage-backed securities held to maturity are summarized as follows:

	December 31, 1993			
	Amortized Cost	Gross Unrealized Gains	Gross Unrealized Losses	Estimated Market Value
		(in thousands)		
GNMA certificates	$20,166	$1,117	$ 3	$21,280
FNMA certificates	587	32	—	619
Non-agency	30,307	944	7	31,244
	$51,060	$2,093	$10	$53,143

	December 31, 1992			
	Amortized Cost	Gross Unrealized Gains	Gross Unrealized Losses	Estimated Market Value
		(in thousands)		
GNMA certificates	$25,804	$ 806	$ 22	$26,588
FNMA certificates	1,497	77	—	1,574
Non-agency	22,038	1,403	—	23,441
	$49,339	$2,286	$ 22	$51,603

Proceeds, gross realized gains and losses on the sales of mortgage-backed securities are summarized as follows:

	1993	1992	1991
		(in thousands)	
Proceeds	$1,040	$326,883	$204,774
Gross realized gains	$ 44	$ 987	$ 437
Gross realized losses	$ —	$ (4,371)	$ (2,844)

Gross realized losses in 1992 includes a $3,584,000 loss on an adjustable rate, AA rated, mortgage-backed security which was purchased by Downey in December, 1991, for $245,468,000 and was classified as held for trading at December 31, 1991. Net unrealized gains (losses) on mortgage-backed securities held for sale recognized in a valuation allowance by charges to net gains on sales of loans and mortgage-backed securities for the years ended December 31, 1993 and 1992, were $0 and $(11,000), respectively.

NBB BANCORP INC., DECEMBER 31, 1994

NBB Bancorp, Inc. and Subsidiary
Consolidated Balance Sheets
(in thousands, except share data)

	December 31,	
	1993	1992

Assets:

. . . .

	December 31,	
	1993	1992
Securities available-for-sale: at fair value in 1993 and lower of cost or market in 1992 (cost of $576,790 in 1993; market value of $417,910 in 1992)	588,442	415,597
Securities held-to-maturity: market value of $409,713 and $443,264	399,453	432,977

. . . .

Stockholders' equity:

. . . .

| Unrealized appreciation on securities available-for-sale, net | 6,772 | — |

. . . .

NBB Bancorp, Inc. and Subsidiary
Consolidated Statements of Income
(in thousands, except share data)

| | Years Ended December 31, | | |
| | 1993 | 1992 | 1991 |

. . . .

Non-Interest Income:

. . . .

| Gain on sales of securities, net | 3,859 | 5,377 | 9,647 |

. . . .

NBB Bancorp, Inc. and Subsidiary
Consolidated Statements of Stockholders' Equity
Years Ended December 31, 1993, 1992, and 1991
(in thousands, except share data)

	Net Unrealized Appreciation on Securities Available-for-Sale
Balance at December 31, 1992	—
Unrealized appreciation on securities available-for-sale, net of deferred income tax expense of $4,880	6,772
Balance at December 31, 1993	$6,772

41

NBB Bancorp, Inc. and Subsidiary
Notes to Consolidated Financial Statements
Years Ended December 31, 1993, 1992, and 1991

1. Summary of Significant Accounting Policies

. . . .

Securities. Effective December 31, 1993, the Bank adopted Statement of Financial Accounting Standards (SFAS) No. 115, "Accounting for Certain Investments in Debt and Equity Securities." Under SFAS No. 115, debt securities that the Bank has the positive intent and ability to hold to maturity are classified as held-to-maturity and reported at amortized cost; debt and equity securities that are bought and held principally for the purpose of selling them in the near term are classified as trading and reported at fair value, with unrealized gains and losses included in earnings; and debt and equity securities not classified as either held-to-maturity or trading are classified as available-for-sale and reported at fair value, with unrealized gains and losses excluded from earnings and reported in a separate component of stockholders' equity. The Bank classifies its securities based on the Bank's intention at the time of purchase. The Bank has no securities held for trading. As a result of adoption, as of December 31, 1993, stockholders' equity was increased by approximately $6,772,000, representing the net unrealized gain on securities available-for-sale, less applicable income taxes.

In 1992 and prior periods, debt securities intended to be held to maturity were carried at amortized cost; marketable equity securities were carried at the lower of aggregate cost or market value; and securities available-for-sale were carried at the lower of cost or market value.

Premiums and discounts on debt securities are amortized or accreted to income by use of the level-yield method. If a decline in fair value below the amortized cost basis of a security is judged to be other than temporary, the cost basis of the investment is written down to fair value as a new cost basis and the amount of the write-down is included in earnings. Gains and losses on the sale of securities are recognized at the time of sale on a specific identification basis.

. . . .

2. Securities Available-for-Sale and Held-to-Maturity

As discussed in Note 1, effective December 31, 1993, the Bancorp adopted SFAS No. 115, "Accounting for Certain Investments in Debt and Equity Securities." The amortized cost and estimated market values of securities available-for-sale and securities held-to-maturity are as follows:

(in thousands)	December 31, 1993			
	Amortized Cost	Gross Unrealized Gains	Gross Unrealized Losses	Estimated Market Value
Securities Available-for-Sale:				
U.S. Government and Federal agency obligations	$503,559	$11,629	$(1,132)	$514,056
Debt securities issued by foreign governments	5,000	5	—	5,005
Corporate debt securities	60	14	—	74
Mortgage-backed securities	40,826	711	(317)	41,220
Marketable equity securities	15,314	1,514	(772)	16,056
Other equity securities	12,031	—	—	12,031
Total securities available-for-sale	$576,790	$13,873	$(2,221)	$588,442

42

(*in thousands*)	December 31, 1993			
	Amortized Cost	Gross Unrealized Gains	Gross Unrealized Losses	Estimated Market Value
Securities Held-to-Maturity:				
U.S. Government and Federal agency obligations	$ 2,575	$ —	$ (7)	$ 2,568
Debt securities issued by political subdivisions of states	160	—	—	160
Debt securities issued by foreign governments	—	—	—	—
Corporate debt securities	121,749	5,600	(27)	127,322
Mortgage-backed securities	25,136	193	(18)	25,311
Other debt securities	249,833	4,963	(444)	254,352
Marketable equity securities	—	—	—	—
Total securities held-to-maturity	$399,453	$10,756	$ (496)	$409,713

(*in thousands*)	December 31, 1992			
	Amortized Cost	Gross Unrealized Gains	Gross Unrealized Losses	Estimated Market Value
Securities Available-for-Sale:				
U.S. Government and Federal agency obligations	$406,627	$3,899	$(1,586)	$408,940
Debt securities issued by foreign governments	—	—	—	—
Corporate debt securities	—	—	—	—
Mortgage-backed securities	—	—	—	—
Marketable equity securities	—	—	—	—
Other equity securities	8,970	—	—	8,970
Total securities available-for-sale	$415,597	$3,899	$(1,586)	$417,910
Securities Held-to-Maturity:				
U.S. Government and Federal agency obligations	$ 47,198	$ 2,480	$ (12)	$ 49,666
Debt securities issued by political subdivisions of states	—	—	—	—
Debt securities issued by foreign governments	3,000	—	—	3,000
Corporate debt securities	118,640	4,210	(117)	122,733
Mortgage-backed securities	37,646	464	(304)	37,806
Other debt securities	210,386	4,071	(902)	213,555
Marketable equity securities	16,107	1,226	(829)	16,504
Total securities held-to-maturity	$432,977	$12,451	$(2,164)	$443,264

The amortized cost and estimated market value of debt securities at December 31, 1993, by contractual maturity, are shown below. Expected maturities may differ from contractual maturities because of prepayments on mortgage-backed securities and certain obligors have the right to call obligations without prepayment penalties.

(*in thousands*)	Securities Available-for-Sale	
	Amortized Cost	Estimated Market Value
Due in one year or less	$ 37,080	$ 37,397
Due after one year through five years	446,232	455,951
Due after five years through ten years	31,247	31,640
Due after ten years	34,886	35,367
Total	$549,445	$560,355

(*in thousands*)	Securities Held-to-Maturity	
	Amortized Cost	Estimated Market Value
Due in one year or less	$100,642	$101,904
Due after one year through five years	266,489	274,855
Due after five years through ten years	6,883	7,340
Due after ten years	25,439	25,614
Total	$399,453	$409,713

Proceeds from sales of securities available-for-sale during 1993, 1992 and 1991 were $248,572,000, $489,152,000 and $655,730,000, respectively. Gross gains of $2,857,000, $6,402,000 and $8,689,000 and gross losses of $40,000, $1,605,000 and $55,000 were realized on those sales.

Proceeds from sales of debt securities held-to-maturity during 1992 and 1991 were $8,217,000 and $30,595,000, respectively. Gross gains of $59,000 and $382,000 and gross losses of $148,000 and $73,000 were realized on those sales. There were no sales of debt securities held-to-maturity in 1993. Proceeds from the sales of equity securities during 1993, 1992 and 1991 were $9,363,000, $11,347,000 and $17,934,000, respectively. Gross gains of $1,586,000, $1,268,000 and $2,282,000 and gross losses of $192,000, $599,000 and $853,000 were realized on those sales. Included in net realized gains for the years ended December 31, 1993 and 1991 are write-downs of $352,000 and $254,000, respectively, in certain equity securities and $471,000 in 1991 in certain debt securities, which represented other than temporary declines in value.

. . . .

FINANCIAL ENTERPRISES OTHER THAN BANKS

Financial enterprises other than banks also have investments in debt and equity securities that must be accounted for in accordance with FASB Statement No. 115. Examples of such accounting in accordance with FASB Statement No. 115 by eight such enterprises are presented below. The examples are classified according to which of these types of financial enterprises is the primary component of the disclosing enterprise:

- Personal or business credit institutions

- Finance services

- Life or accident and health insurance companies

- Fire, marine, or casualty insurance companies

PERSONAL OR BUSINESS CREDIT INSTITUTIONS

FOOTHILL GROUP INC., DECEMBER 31, 1993

The Foothill Group, Inc.
Consolidated Balance Sheets

| | Years Ended December 31, | |
	1993	1992
Assets		
. . . .		
Equity, debt and partnership investments	32,842,000	13,992,000

45

Consolidated Balance Sheets (continued)

	Years Ended December 31,	
	1993	1992

. . . .

Stockholders' equity (Note 5):

. . . .

Unrealized gains on securities available for sale	19,672,000	—

. . . .

The Foothill Group, Inc.
Consolidated Statements of Income
Years Ended December 31, 1993, 1992, and 1991

	Year Ended December 31,		
	1993	1992	1991

. . . .

Revenues (Note 1):

. . . .

Gain on investments, net	5,257,000	3,373,000	1,022,000

. . . .

The Foothill Group, Inc.
Consolidated Statements of Stockholders' Equity
Years Ended December 31, 1993, 1992, and 1991

	Unrealized Gain on Securities Available for Sale
Balances at December 31, 1992	—
Unrealized gains on securities available for sale (Note 10)	19,672,000
Balances at December 31, 1993	$19,672,000

The Foothill Group, Inc.
Notes to Consolidated Financial Statements
Years Ended December 31, 1993, 1992, and 1991

Note 1. Summary of Significant Accounting Policies

. . . .

   Equity, Debt and Partnership Investments. Equity securities were primarily received as a result of exchanges of private placements and discounted receivables for new securities of the reorganized debtors. At December 31, 1993, the Company adopted the requirements of FASB Statement No. 115, "Accounting for Certain Investments in Debt and Equity Securities," and classified its marketable debt and equity securities as "available for sale." Accordingly, these securities have been marked-to-market, with the increase in their carrying value, net of income taxes, included as a component of stockholder's equity. The Company has recorded valuation adjustments in cases where an "other than temporary" impairment in estimated net realizable value below the Company's cost basis in investments is believed to have occurred.

For the years ended December 1993, 1992 and 1991, there were gross realized gains of $282,000, $1,275,000 and $506,000 and gross realized losses of $0, $33,000 and $2,924,000, respectively, resulting from sales of these equity securities whose gross sales proceeds totaled $761,000, $2,064,000 and $3,462,000, respectively. Included in the 1993, 1992 and 1991 proceeds are cash proceeds of $634,000, $1,950,000 and $2,647,000, respectively, and noncash proceeds of $127,000, $114,000 and $815,000 in 1993, 1992 and 1991, respectively, which resulted from investment reorganizations or exchanges.

. . . .

HOUSEHOLD INTERNATIONAL INC., DECEMBER 31, 1993

Household International, Inc. and Subsidiaries
Statements of Income
(all dollar amounts except per share data are stated in millions.)

	Year Ended December 31,		
	1993	1992	1991
. . . .			
Investment income	574.0	523.7	471.5

. . . .

Household International, Inc. and Subsidiaries
Balance Sheets
(in millions)

	December 31,	
	1993	1992
Assets		
. . . .		
Investment securities (fair value of $9,045.5 and $7,633.4)	8,795.1	7,389.8

. . . .

Household International, Inc. and Subsidiaries
Statements of Changes in Preferred Stock and Common Shareholders' Equity
(all dollar amounts are stated in millions.)

	Other [2]
Balance at December 31, 1992	(804.5)

	Other [2]
. . . .	
Unrealized gain on investments, net (4)	44.5
. . . .	
Balance at December 31, 1993	$(548.6)

. . . .

(2) At December 31, 1993, 1992, 1991 and 1990, items in the other column include cumulative adjustments for: .... unrealized gains (losses) on marketable equity securities and available-for-sale investments of $40.5, $(4.0), $(3.1), and $(9.9) million, respectively; ....

. . . .

(4) Effective December 31, 1993, the company adopted Statement of Financial Accounting Standards No. 115, "Accounting for Certain Investments in Debt and Equity Securities" ("FAS No. 115"). As a result of implementing FAS No. 115, the gross unrealized gain on available-for-sale investments of $152.8 million is recorded net of income taxes of $22.1 million and, for certain available-for-sale investments of the life insurance operation, related unrealized deferred insurance policy acquisition cost adjustments of $90.2 million at December 31, 1993.

Notes to Financial Statements
Household International, Inc. and Subsidiaries

1. Summary of Significant Accounting Policies

. . . .

Investment Securities. The company maintains investment portfolios in both its noninsurance and insurance operations. These portfolios are comprised primarily of debt securities. The insurance portfolio also includes mortgage and policyholder loans and other real estate investments. Effective December 31, 1993 the company adopted Statement of Financial Accounting Standards No. 115, "Accounting for Certain Investments in Debt and Equity Securities" ("FAS No. 115"). In accordance with FAS No. 115, investment securities in both the noninsurance and insurance operations are classified in three separate categories: trading, available-for-sale or held-to-maturity. Trading investments are brought and held principally for the purpose of selling them in the near term and are carried at fair value. Adjustments to the carrying value of trading investments are included in current earnings. Investments in which the company has the positive intent and ability to hold to maturity are classified as held-to-maturity and carried at amortized cost. Investments not classified as trading or held-to-maturity are classified as available-for-sale. They are intended to be invested for an indefinite period but may be sold in response to events reasonably expected in the foreseeable future. These investments are carried at fair value. Unrealized holding gains and losses on available-for-sale investments are recorded as adjustments to common shareholders' equity, net of income taxes and, for certain investments of the insurance operation, related unrealized deferred insurance policy acquisition cost adjustments (see "Insurance" on the following page). Prior to the adoption of FAS No. 115, available-for-sale investments were carried at the lower of aggregate amortized cost or fair value, and any adjustments to carrying value for the noninsurance operations were included in earnings, while any adjustments to carrying value for the insurance operations were included in common shareholders' equity. Any decline in the fair value of available-for-sale or held-to-maturity investments which is deemed to be other than temporary is charged against current earnings.

Cost of investment securities sold by the insurance operation generally is determined using the first-in, first-out ("FIFO") method, and cost of noninsurance investment securities sold is determined by specific identification. Interest income earned on the noninsurance investment portfolio is classified in the statements of income in net interest margin. Realized gains and losses from the noninsurance portfolio and investment income from the insurance portfolio are recorded in investment income. Gains and losses on trading investments are recorded in other income. Accrued investment income is classified with investment securities.

. . . .

2. Investment Securities

(in millions) At December 31	1993	
	Carrying Value	Fair Value
Trading Investments		
Government securities and other	$ 108.8	$ 108.8
Available-for-Sale Investments		
Marketable equity securities:		
Common stocks	18.5	18.5
Preferred stocks	66.3	66.3
Corporate securities	2,047.1	2,047.1
Government securities	536.3	536.3
Mortgage-backed securities	1,983.9	1,983.9
Other	347.8	347.8
Subtotal	4,999.9	4,999.9
Held-to-Maturity Investments		
Corporate securities	1,852.3	2,049.4
Government securities	34.5	36.7
Mortgage-backed securities	882.1	928.1
Mortgage loans on real estate	222.4	226.0
Policy loans	81.6	81.6
Other	494.6	496.1
Subtotal	3,567.5	3,817.9
Accrued investment income	118.9	118.9
Total investment securities	$8,795.1	$9,045.5

(in millions) At December 31	1992	
	Carrying Value	Fair Value
Trading Investments		
Government securities and other	$ 39.8	$ 39.8
Available-for-Sale Investments		
Marketable equity securities:		
Common stocks	10.8	10.8
Preferred stocks	85.8	85.8
Corporate securities	323.8	323.8
Government securities	82.3	82.3

2. Investment Securities (continued)

(in millions) At December 31	1992	
	Carrying Value	Fair Value
Mortgage-backed securities	634.7	648.9
Other	—	—
Subtotal	1,136.9	1,151.1
Held-to-Maturity Investments		
Corporate securities	2,956.8	3,104.7
Government securities	181.7	186.9
Mortgage-backed securities	2,024.5	2,084.8
Mortgage loans on real estate	351.0	365.7
Policy loans	75.2	75.2
Other	508.2	509.5
Subtotal	6,097.4	6,326.8
Accrued investment income	115.7	115.7
Total investment securities	$7,389.8	$7,633.4

The company's insurance subsidiaries held $6.7 and $5.7 billion of the investment securities at December 31, 1993 and 1992, respectively. Policy loans and mortgage loans on real estate held by the company's insurance subsidiaries are classified as investment securities, consistent with insurance industry practice.

Included in the company's earnings for 1993, 1992 and 1991 were changes in net unrealized holding gains (losses) of $1.3, $(3.3) and $6.6 million, respectively, from trading investments.

Proceeds from the sale of available-for-sale investments totaled approximately $1.2 billion in both 1993 and 1992. Gross gains of $49.7 and $31.1 million and gross losses of $7.9 and $21.9 million in 1993 and 1992, respectively, were realized on those sales. There were no investments classified as available-for-sale in 1991.

The amortized cost of held-to-maturity investments transferred to available-for-sale in 1993 was $3.7 billion. Proceeds from sales of held-to-maturity investments were $834.3 million, $871.4 million and $2.2 billion during 1993, 1992 and 1991, respectively. Sales and transfers of held-to-maturity investments in 1993 were due to restructuring of the investment security portfolio in anticipation of the adoption of FAS No. 115 on December 31, 1993. Approximately $400 and $800 million of sales proceeds in 1992 and 1991 were related to a decision made in 1991 to restructure held-to-maturity investments to significantly reduce exposure in the company's non-investment grade bond portfolio. Gross gains of $48.1, $35.4 and $59.3 million and gross losses of $9.6, $15.9 a $28.0 million were realized on sales of held-to-maturity investments in 1993, 1992 and 1991, respectively.

The gross unrealized gains (losses) on investment securities were as follows:

(in millions) At December 31	1993			
	Amortized Cost	Gross Unrealized Gains	Gross Unrealized Losses	Fair Value
Available-for-Sale Investments				
Marketable equity securities:				
Common stocks	$ 16.9	$ 1.7	$ (.1)	$ 18.5
Preferred stocks	63.8	4.2	(1.7)	66.3
Corporate securities	1,960.4	95.9	(9.2)	2,047.1
Government securities	531.9	6.3	(1.9)	536.3
Mortgage-backed securities	1,926.3	63.2	(5.6)	1,983.9

(in millions) At December 31	1993 Amortized Cost	Gross Unrealized Gains	Gross Unrealized Losses	Fair Value
Other	347.8	—	—	347.8
Total available-for-sale investments	$4,847.1	$171.3	$(18.5)	$4,999.9
Held-to-Maturity Investments				
Corporate securities	$1,852.3	$202.9	$ (5.8)	$2,049.4
Government securities	34.5	2.2	—	36.7
Mortgage-backed securities	882.1	48.5	(2.5)	928.1
Mortgage loans on real estate	222.4	6.2	(2.6)	226.0
Policy loans	81.6	—	—	81.6
Other	494.6	1.5	—	496.1
Total held-to-maturity investments	$3,567.5	$261.3	$(10.9)	$3,817.9

(in millions) At December 31	1992 Amortized Cost	Gross Unrealized Gains	Gross Unrealized Losses	Fair Value
Available-for-Sale Investments				
Marketable equity securities:				
Common stocks	$ 10.1	$ .8	$ (.1)	$ 10.8
Preferred stocks	89.6	2.1	(5.9)	85.8
Corporate securities	324.3	11.0	(12.0)	323.3
Government securities	79.2	3.2	(.1)	82.3
Mortgage-backed securities	638.6	15.1	(4.8)	648.9
Other	—	—	—	—
Total available-for-sale investments	$1,141.8	$32.2	$(22.9)	$1,151.1
Held-to-Maturity Investments				
Corporate securities	$2,956.8	$154.5	$ (6.6)	$3,104.7
Government securities	181.7	5.6	(.4)	186.9
Mortgage-backed securities	2,024.5	69.9	(9.6)	2,084.8
Mortgage loans on real estate	351.0	18.8	(4.1)	365.7
Policy loans	75.2	—	—	75.2
Other	508.2	1.5	(.2)	509.5
Total held-to-maturity investments	$6,097.4	$250.3	$(20.9)	$6,326.8

. . . .

Contractual maturities and yields of investments in debt securities available-for-sale and held-to-maturity were as follows:

(in millions) At December 31, 1993	Corporate Securities Amortized Cost	Fair Value	Yield (*)
Available-for-Sale Investments			
Due within 1 year	$ 7.3	$ 7.5	8.10%
After 1 but within 5 years	139.0	145.2	7.51

2. Investment Securities (continued)

(*in millions*) At December 31, 1993	Corporate Securities		
	Amortized Cost	Fair Value	Yield (*)
After 5 but within 10 years	1,151.4	1,194.7	7.43
After 10 years	662.7	699.7	7.70
Total	$1,960.4	$2,047.1	7.53%
Held-to-Maturity Investments			
Due within 1 year	$ 67.0	$ 68.3	10.61%
After 1 but within 5 years	276.2	304.3	9.57
After 5 but within 10 years	447.2	4,963.9	8.83
After 10 years	1,061.9	1,179.9	8.78
Total	$1,852.3	$2,049.4	8.98%

(*in millions*) At December 31, 1993	Government Securities		
	Amortized Cost	Fair Value	Yield (*)
Available-for-Sale Investments			
Due within 1 year	$ 206.6	$ 206.9	4.35%
After 1 but within 5 years	152.1	153.7	5.06
After 5 but within 10 years	153.3	153.6	5.88
After 10 years	19.9	22.1	8.04
Total	$ 531.9	$ 536.3	5.13%
Held-to-Maturity Investments			
Due within 1 year	$ 2.3	$ 2.4	6.44%
After 1 but within 5 years	3.6	3.7	5.88
After 5 but within 10 years	16.2	17.0	6.66
After 10 years	12.4	13.6	9.69
Total	$34.5	$36.7	7.65%

(*in millions*) At December 31, 1993	All Other Debt Securities		
	Amortized Cost	Fair Value	Yield (*)
Available-for-Sale Investments			
Due within 1 year	$ 545.0	$ 543.8	3.76%
After 1 but within 5 years	—	—	—
After 5 but within 10 years	162.2	171.0	8.08
After 10 years	1,294.8	1,344.8	6.73
Total	$2,002.0	$2,059.6	6.03%
Held-to-Maturity Investments			
Due within 1 year	$ 10.7	$ 10.7	4.62%
After 1 but within 5 years	—	—	—
After 5 but within 10 years	148.8	157.7	6.60
After 10 years	868.9	907.4	8.59
Total	$1,028.4	$1,075.8	8.26%

(*) Computed by dividing annualized interest by the amortized cost of the respective investment securities.

52

FINANCE SERVICES

AMERICAN FINANCIAL CORPORATION, DECEMBER 31, 1993

American Financial Corporation
Consolidated Balance Sheet

	(*in thousands*) As of December 31,	
	1993	1992
Assets		
. . . .		
Investments:		
Bonds and redeemable preferred stocks:		
Held to maturity — at amortized cost		
(market — $3,959,400 and $4,705,600)	3,788,732	4,597,544
Available for sale — at market (amortized cost —		
$2,216,328 and $1,905,814)	2,349,528	1,976,514
Other stocks — principally at market		
(cost — $207,056 and $182,476)	339,156	230,876
. . . .		
Retained earnings	210,846	42,402
Net unrealized gain on marketable securities,		
net of deferred income taxes	156,900	68,100

. . . .

American Financial Corporation
Consolidated Statement of Operations

	(*in thousands*) Year Ended December 31,		
	1993	1992	1991
Income:			
. . . .			
Realized gains on sales of securities	82,265	101,474	50,795
. . . .			
Provision for impairment of investments	(1,500)	(2,000)	(37,822)

. . . .

American Financial Corporation
Consolidated Statement of Changes in Capital Accounts
(in thousands)

| | Year Ended December 31, | | |
	1993	1992	1991
Net Unrealized Gain on Marketable Securities, Net of Deferred Income Taxes:			
Balance at beginning of period	$ 68,100	$ 2,700	$ 47,100
Change during period	88,800	65,400	(44,400)
Balance at End of Period	$156,900	$68,100	$ 2,700

American Financial Corporation
Notes to Consolidated Financial Statements

A. Accounting Policies

. . . .

Investments. AFC implemented Statement of Financial Accounting Standards ("SFAS") No. 115, "Accounting for Certain Investments in Debt and Equity Securities," beginning December 31, 1993. This standard requires (i) debt securities be classified as "held to maturity" and reported at amortized cost if AFC has the positive intent and ability to hold them to maturity, (ii) debt and equity securities be classified as "trading" and reported at fair value, with unrealized gains and losses included in earnings, if they are bought and held principally for selling in the near term and (iii) debt and equity securities not classified as held to maturity or trading be classified as "available for sale" and reported at fair value, with unrealized gains and losses reported as a separate component of shareholders' equity. Only in certain limited circumstances, such as significant issuer credit deterioration or if required by insurance or other regulators, may a company change its intent to hold a certain security to maturity without calling into question its intent to hold other debt securities to maturity in the future.

Effective September 30, 1992, AFC had reclassified its portfolio of bonds and redeemable preferred stocks into two categories, held to maturity and available for sale, and accounted for them in a manner similar to that required by SFAS No. 115. In connection with implementing SFAS No. 115, AFC made a comprehensive review of its investment portfolio. This review resulted in a reclassification of approximately $704 million of its fixed maturity portfolio (including $485 million in CMOs) from "held to maturity" to "available for sale" which, in turn, resulted in (i) an increase of $36 million in the carrying value of fixed maturity investments, and (ii) an increase of $19 million in AFC's shareholders' equity. The reclassification reflected management's intention to reduce the proportion of CMOs owned and more actively manage the duration of its fixed income portfolio. Implementation of SFAS No. 115 had no effect on net earnings.

Premiums and discounts on collateralized mortgage obligations are amortized over their expected average lives using the interest method. Gains or losses on sales of securities are recognized at the time of disposition with the amount of gain or loss determined on the specific identification basis. When a decline in the value of a specific investment is considered to be other than temporary, a provision for impairment is charged to earnings and the carrying value of that investment is reduced.

. . . .

D. Investments

Bonds, redeemable preferred stocks and other stocks at December 31, consisted of the following (*in millions*):

1993	Held to Maturity			
	Amortized Cost	Market Value	Gross Unrealized	
			Gains	Losses
Bonds and Redeemable Preferred Stocks:				
United States Government and government agencies and authorities	$ —	$ —	$ —	$ —
States, municipalities and political subdivisions	26.9	28.8	1.9	—
Foreign government	24.9	23.9	.9	(1.9)
Public utilities	623.8	643.4	24.1	(4.5)
CMO's	703.5	717.7	18.4	(4.2)
All other corporate	2,314.0	2,447.3	141.0	(7.7)
Redeemable preferred stocks	95.6	98.3	2.9	(.2)
	$3,788.7	$3,959.4	$189.2	($18.5)

1993	Available for Sale			
	Amortized Cost	Market Value	Gross Unrealized	
			Gains	Losses
Bonds and Redeemable Preferred Stocks:				
United States Government and government agencies and authorities	$ 208.0	$ 217.1	$ 9.1	$ —
States, municipalities and political subdivisions	35.0	37.3	2.3	—
Foreign government	15.7	15.7	—	—
Public utilities	135.9	141.2	5.3	—
CMO's	1,129.0	1,183.3	54.3	—
All other corporate	692.7	754.9	62.2	—
Redeemable preferred stocks	—	—	—	—
	$2,216.3	$2,349.5	$133.2	$ —
Other stocks	$ 207.1	$ 339.2	$137.2	($ 5.1)

1992	Held to Maturity			
	Amortized Cost	Market Value	Gross Unrealized	
			Gains	Losses
Bonds and Redeemable Preferred Stocks:				
United States Government and government agencies and authorities	$ 86.5	$ 87.0	$ .5	$ —
States, municipalities and political subdivisions	52.9	55.1	2.9	(.7)
Foreign government	22.7	19.3	—	(3.4)
Public utilities	742.1	761.9	20.7	(.9)
CMO's	1,176.6	1,197.1	24.5	(4.0)

D. Investments (continued)

1992

	Held to Maturity			
	Amortized Cost	Market Value	Gross Unrealized	
			Gains	Losses
All other corporate	2,447.0	2,512.5	78.0	(12.5)
Redeemable preferred stocks	69.7	72.7	3.0	—
	$4,597.5	$4,705.6	$129.6	($21.5)

1992

	Available for Sale			
	Amortized Cost	Market Value	Gross Unrealized	
			Gains	Losses
Bonds and Redeemable Preferred Stocks:				
United States Government and government agencies and authorities	$ 430.4	$ 441.6	$ 11.2	$ —
States, municipalities and political subdivisions	—	—	—	—
Foreign government	—	—	—	—
Public utilities	25.1	25.9	.8	—
CMO's	878.8	919.6	41.6	(.8)
All other corporate	571.5	589.4	21.9	(4.0)
Redeemable preferred stocks	—	—	—	—
	$1,905.8	$1,976.5	$75.5	($ 4.8)

The table below sets forth the scheduled maturities of bonds and redeemable preferred stocks based on carrying value as of December 31, 1993. Data based on market value is generally the same. Collateralized mortgage obligations have an average life of approximately 4 years at December 31, 1993.

Maturity	Held to Maturity	Available for Sale
One year or less	1%	1%
After one year through five years	7	5
After five years through ten years	18	13
After ten years	55	31
	81	50
Collateralized mortgage obligations	19	50
	100%	100%

Gross gains of $69.4 million, $85.2 million and $208.8 million and gross losses of $16.5 million, $4.7 million and $236.9 million were realized on sales of fixed maturity investments during 1993, 1992, and 1991, respectively.

Realized gains (losses) and changes in unrealized appreciation (depreciation) on fixed maturity and equity security investments are summarized as follows (*in thousands*):

1993	Fixed Maturities	Equity Securities	Tax Effects	Total
Realized	$ 52,915	$ 29,350	($ 28,793)	$ 53,472
Change in Unrealized	125,112	83,700	(73,084)	135,728

56

	Fixed Maturities	Equity Securities	Tax Effects	Total
1992				
Realized	80,503	20,971	(34,501)	66,973
Change in Unrealized	(78,293)	44,300	11,558	(22,435)
1991				
Realized	(28,076)	78,871	(17,270)	33,525
Change in Unrealized	349,596	(67,200)	(96,015)	186,381

Investment in other stocks at December 31, 1992 consisted of (*in thousands*):

	Cost	Market	Reporting Value
Insurance companies' portfolios	$ 178,055	$ 226,455	$ 226,455
Other companies' portfolios	4,421	4,633	4,421
	$182,476	$231,088	$230,876

At December 31, 1992, gross unrealized gains on other stocks were $63.7 million and gross unrealized losses were $15.1 million.

Carrying values of investments were determined after deducting cumulative provisions for impairment aggregating $47 million and $78 million at December 31, 1993 and 1992, respectively.

Fair values for investments are based on prices quoted, when available, in the most active market for each security. If quoted prices are not available, fair value is estimated based on present values, fair values of comparable securities, or similar methods.

Short-term investments are carried at cost; loans receivable are stated at the aggregate unpaid balance. Carrying amounts of these investments approximate their fair value.

MIDLAND COMPANY, DECEMBER 31, 1993

Consolidated Balance Sheets
The Midland Company and Subsidiaries

December 31,	1993	1992
Assets		
. . . .		
Marketable Securities	224,614,000	188,531,000
. . . .		
Shareholders' Equity:		
. . . .		
Net unrealized gain on marketable securities	11,308,000	5,836,000
. . . .		

The Midland Company and Subsidiaries
Notes to Consolidated Financial Statements
Years Ended December 31, 1993, 1992, and 1991

1. Summary of Significant Accounting Policies

. . . .

Marketable Securities — Marketable securities are categorized as debt securities (cash equivalents, debt instruments and preferred stocks having scheduled redemption provisions) and equity securities (common stocks and preferred stocks which do not have redemption provisions). The Company adopted Statement of Financial Accounting Standards (SFAS) No. 115, "Accounting for Certain Investments in Debt and Equity Securities," effective December 31, 1993 (also see note 2). This statement requires securities to be classified as trading, available-for-sale or held-to-maturity. Only those debt securities classified as held-to-maturity are carried at amortized cost, while those debt and equity securities classified as trading or available-for-sale are carried at market value. At December 31, 1993, all debt and equity securities are classified as available-for-sale and are carried at market value. Prior to 1993, debt securities were carried at amortized cost, equity securities held by the insurance subsidiaries were carried at market value, and equity securities held by the parent company were carried at the lower of cost or market value.

2. Marketable Securities

1993	Cost	Gross Unrealized Gains	Gross Unrealized Losses	Market Value
Debt Securities:				
Governments	$ 69,482	$ 3,101	$ 106	$ 72,477
Municipals	61,642	3,475	119	64,998
Cash Equivalents	45,965	—	—	45,965
Corporates	10,514	467	4	10,977
Total	187,603	7,043	229	194,417
Equity Securities	16,864	11,117	639	27,342
Accrued Interest and Dividends	2,855	—	—	2,855
Total Marketable Securities	$207,322	$18,160	$ 868	$224,614

(thousands of dollars)

1992	Gains	Market Value	Carrying Value
Debt Securities:			
Governments	$ 71,114	$ 75,200	$ 71,114
Municipals	51,478	53,514	51,478
Cash Equivalents	30,633	30,633	30,633
Corporates	7,774	8,101	7,774
Total	160,999	167,448	160,999
Equity Securities:			
Parent Co.	2,097	4,033	2,097

(thousands of dollars)

	Gains	Market Value	Carrying Value
Insurance Subs.	14,588	22,514	22,514
Total	16,685	26,547	24,611
Accrued Interest and Dividends	2,921	2,921	2,921
Total Marketable Securities	$180,605	$196,916	$188,531

(thousands of dollars)

Gross unrealized gains and losses on Marketable Securities as of December 31, 1992 were (*amounts in 000's*):

	Gains	Losses
Debt Securities:		
Governments	$ 4,238	$152
Municipals	2,079	43
Corporates	331	4
Total	$ 6,648	$199
Equity Securities:		
Parent Co.	$ 1,941	$ 5
Insurance Subs.	8,354	428
Total	$10,295	$433

The net unrealized gains and losses on marketable securities carried at market value are included in a valuation allowance in Shareholders' Equity. In 1992, this valuation allowance also included $916,000 of unrealized gains on appreciated equity securities purchased by the parent company from an insurance subsidiary. The valuation allowance is net of deferred federal income taxes of $5,984,000 in 1993 and $3,006,000 in 1992. As a result of changes in this valuation allowance, Shareholders' Equity increased $5,472,000, $1,556,000 and $3,034,000 in 1993, 1992, and 1991, respectively. Included in the 1993 change in valuation allowance was $6,659,000 which represented the effect of the change in accounting for debt and equity securities (see note 1).

Included in the determination of net income are net realized gains of $3,735,000, $1,510,000 and $631,000 in 1993, 1992, and 1991, respectively. The cost of securities sold is based on specific identification of the securities at the time of sale.

The cost and approximate market value of debt securities at December 31, 1993, by contractual maturities, are shown below. Actual maturities may differ from contractual maturities when there exists a right to call or prepay obligations with or without call or prepayment penalties (*amounts in 000's*).

	Cost	Market Value
Debt Securities:		
Under 1 year	$ 52,204	$ 52,347
1–5 years	100,328	104,811
6–10 years	31,177	33,365
Over 10 years	3,894	3,894
	$187,603	$194,417

LIFE OR ACCIDENT AND HEALTH INSURANCE COMPANIES

AMERICAN INDEMNITY FINANCIAL CORPORATION, DECEMBER 31, 1993

Consolidated Balance Sheets

	December 31,	
	1993	1992 (1)
Assets		
Investments:		
Fixed maturities — bonds:		
Held for investment (approximate		
market value $36,863,470 in 1992)	$	$36,334,545
Available for sale (amortized cost $68,644,151		
in 1993 and approximate market value		
$29,195,574 in 1992)	69,277,292	28,845,916
Equity securities:		
Preferred stocks — at market value (cost $2,395,586		
in 1993 and $2,513,551 in 1992)	2,467,528	2,495,108
Common stocks — at market value (cost $16,216,716		
in 1993 and $12,029,812 in 1992)	17,410,880	13,048,328
. . . .		
Accrued Investment Income	1,136,046	876,879
. . . .		
Stockholders' Equity:		
. . . .		
Unrealized appreciation in market value of investments	1,892,790	985,470
. . . .		

Consolidated Statements of Income

	For the Years Ended December 31,		
	1993	1992	1991
. . . .			
Net investment income	5,252,684	5,535,826	5,650,067
Realized investment gains (losses)	1,274,693	1,360,140	(5,039)
. . . .			

60

Consolidated Statements of Stockholders' Equity
For the Three Years Ended December 31, 1993

	Unrealized Appreciation (Decline) in Market Value of Investments
Balance, December 31, 1992	985,470
Change in market value of investments	274,179
Effect of restatement of bonds as of December 31, 1993 from lower of the aggregate amortized cost or market value to market value (Note 2)	633,141
Common stock issued in connection with stock option plans	
Balance, December 31, 1993	$1,892,790

Notes to Consolidated Financial Statements
For the Three Years Ended December 31, 1993

1. Summary of Significant Accounting and Reporting Policies

. . . .

Investments. Fixed maturities are purchased to support the investment strategies of the Company, which are based on many factors including rate of return, maturity, credit risk, tax considerations and regulatory requirements. Effective December 31, 1993, the Company adopted Statement of Financial Accounting Standards No. 115, "Accounting for Certain Investments in Debt and Equity Securities." This statement addresses the accounting and reporting for investments in equity securities that have readily determinable fair values and for all investments in debt securities. The adoption of this standard resulted in the reclassification of all bonds not already classified as available for sale, as available for sale and the reporting of all bonds at market value. Unrealized gains and losses have been excluded from earnings and reported as a net amount in a separate component of stockholders' equity. The effect of the adoption of this standard was an increase to stockholders' equity of approximately $ 633,000 at December 31, 1993 as the aggregate market value of these securities exceeded their amortized cost.

Investments in equity securities are stated at market value.

Unrealized gains or losses on investments which are reported at market value are credited or charged to stockholders' equity, net of a provision for federal income tax, if any. Gains or losses on disposition are computed by the identified certificate method.

. . . .

2. Investments and Investment Income

Fixed Maturities — Bonds. The amortized cost and estimated market values of investments in fixed maturities — bonds are as follows:

	December 31, 1993	
	Amortized Cost	Gross Unrealized Gains
United States Government and Government Agencies and Authorities	$60,818,255	$615,747

2. Investments and Investment Income (continued)

	December 31, 1993	
	Amortized Cost	Gross Unrealized Gains
States, Municipalities and Political Subdivisions	7,663,904	247,460
Public Utilities	25,094	156
All Other Corporate	136,898	5,500
Totals	$68,644,151	$868,863

	December 31, 1993	
	Gross Unrealized Losses	Estimated Market Value
United States Government and Government Agencies and Authorities	$ 225,432	$61,208,570
States, Municipalities and Political Subdivisions	10,017	7,901,347
Public Utilities		25,250
All Other Corporate	273	142,125
Totals	$235,722	$69,277,292

	December 31, 1992	
	Amortized Cost	Gross Unrealized Gains
United States Government and Government Agencies and Authorities:		
Held for investment	$26,273,638	$845,741
Available for sale	26,694,460	499,073
States, Municipalities and Political Subdivisions:		
Held for investment	9,836,528	139,022
Available for sale	1,964,879	19,375
Public Utilities:		
Held for investment	75,131	1,000
Available for sale	62,142	5,018
All Other Corporate:		
Held for investments	152,968	
Available for sale	127,762	14,600
Totals:		
Held for investments	$36,338,265	$985,763
Available for sale	$28,849,243	$538,066

	December 31, 1992	
	Gross Unrealized Losses	Estimated Market Value
United States Government and Government Agencies and Authorities:		
Held for investment	$391,530	$26,727,849
Available for sale	174,904	27,018,629
States, Municipalities and Political Subdivisions:		
Held for investment	66,229	9,909,321

	December 31, 1992	
	Gross Unrealized Losses	Estimated Market Value
Available for sale	16,269	1,967,985
Public Utilities:		
Held for investment	131	76,000
Available for sale		67,160
All Other Corporate:		
Held for investment	2,668	150,300
Available for sale	562	141,800
Totals:		
Held for investment	$460,558	$36,863,470
Available for sale	$191,735	$29,195,574

The amortized cost of bonds held for investment and bonds available for sale for 1992 is $3,720 and $3,327 greater, respectively, than the values shown in the balance sheet as a result of several fixed maturities required to be carried at market value in accordance with National Association of Insurance Commissioners' valuation guidelines. Bonds with an amortized cost of approximately $7,288,000 were on deposit with regulatory authorities at December 31, 1993.

The amortized cost and estimated market value of fixed maturities at December 31, 1993, by scheduled maturity, are shown below. Expected maturities will differ from scheduled maturities because borrowers may have the right to call or prepay obligations with or without call or prepayment penalties.

	December 31, 1993	
Maturity Distribution	Amortized Cost	Estimated Market Value
Due in one year or less	$ 8,028,261	$ 8,201,993
Due after one year through five years	39,360,459	39,736,205
Due after five years through ten years	17,673,022	17,626,465
Due after ten years	3,582,409	3,712,629
Totals	$68,644,151	$69,277,292

Effective December 31, 1993, the Company adopted Statement of Financial Accounting Standards No. 115, "Accounting for Certain Investments in Debt and Equity Securities." This statement addresses the accounting and reporting for investments in equity securities that have readily determinable fair values and for all investments in debt securities. The adoption of this standard resulted in the reclassification of all bonds not already classified for sale as available for sale and the reporting of all bonds at market value. Unrealized gains and losses have been excluded from earnings and reported as a net amount in a separate component of stockholders' equity. The effect of the adoption of this standard was an increase to stockholders' equity of approximately $633,000 at December 31, 1993, as the aggregate market value of these securities exceeded their amortized cost.

Investment Gains and Losses. Realized investment gains and losses and unrealized appreciation or decline in market value of investments are as follows:

	Years Ended December 31,		
	1993	1992	1991
Realized Investment Gains (Losses):			
Fixed maturities — Bonds	$1,013,452	$1,275,172	$(2,647)

2. Investments and Investment Income (continued)

	Years Ended December 31,		
	1993	1992	1991
Equity securities	261,241	84,968	(2,392)
Total	1,274,693	1,360,140	(5,039)
Unrealized Appreciation (Decline) in Market Value of Investments:			
Fixed maturities — Bonds:			
* Eligible	(245,442)	(901,429)	2,720,512
Ineligible	7,047	196,426	42,344
Total	(238,395)	(705,003)	2,762,856
Equity Securities	266,033	246,168	928,832
Total	27,638	(458,835)	3,691,688
Total	$1,302,331	$901,305	$3,686,649

* Prior to 1993, eligible bonds were stated in the balance sheets at amortized cost in compliance with the National Association of Insurance Commissioners' valuation guidelines, whereas ineligible bonds were stated in the balance sheets at market value. For 1993, all bonds are stated in the balance sheet at market value.

Proceeds from sales of investments in fixed maturities — bonds during 1993, 1992 and 1991 were $82,385,020, $33,257,810 and $4,485,076, respectively. The gross realized investment gains and losses for such sales were as follows: Realized investment gains: 1993 — $1,205,604; 1992 — $1,376,992; and 1991 — $29,415. Realized investment losses: 1993 — $208,180; 1992 — $46,918; and 1991 — $24,887. The gross unrealized gains and losses on equity securities at December 31, 1993, were approximately $2,001,000 and $735,000, respectively.

Net Investment Income

	Years Ended December 31,		
	1993	1992	1991
Fixed Maturities — Bonds	$4,318,843	$4,546,205	$5,535,042
Equity Securities:			
Common stocks	798,537	568,099	155,313
Preferred stocks	204,297	507,378	143,183
Mortgage Loans on Real Estate	3,473	3,821	4,135
Other Short-Term Investments	286,053	252,710	149,526
Total Investment Income	5,611,203	5,878,213	5,987,199
Less Investment Expenses	358,519	342,387	337,132
Net Investment Income	$5,252,684	$5,535,826	$5,650,067

ATLANTIC AMERICAN CORPORATION, DECEMBER 31, 1993

Atlantic American Corporation
Consolidated Balance Sheets
The Years Ended December 31
(*in thousands, except share and per share data*)

	1993	1992

. . . .

	1993	1992
Assets		
Insurance		
. . . .		
Investments	84,646	66,092
. . . .		
Shareholders' equity:		
. . . .		
Net unrealized investment gains	10,599	9,456
. . . .		

Atlantic American Corporation
Consolidated Statements of Operations
Year Ended December 31
(in thousands, except share data)

	1993	1992	1991
Insurance Revenue:			
. . . .			
Investment income	5,404	5,696	7,444
Realized investment gains (losses), net	744	4,091	(7,092)
. . . .			

Atlantic American Corporation
Consolidated Statements Of Shareholders' Equity
(in thousands)

	Net Unrealized Investment Gains
Balance, December 31, 1992	9,456
Effect of change in accounting principle for certain investments in debt securities	1,253
Decrease in unrealized investment gains	(110)
Balance, December 31, 1993	$10,599

Notes to Consolidated Financial Statements
The Years Ended December 31, 1993, 1992, and 1991
(dollars in thousands, except share data)

2) Investments — Insurance

Investments are comprised of the following:

	1993	
	Carrying Value	Gross Unrealized Gains
Bonds:		
U.S. Treasury securities and obligations of		
U.S. Government and Corporations and Agencies	$15,939	$ 732
Obligations of states & political subdivisions	2,985	63
Corporate securities	22,199	694
Mortgage-backed securities	1,920	4
	43,043	1,493
Common and preferred stocks	34,391	10,225
Mortgage loans (estimated fair value of $849)	778	
Policy and student loans (1)	6,388	
Real estate	46	
Investments	84,646	
Short-term investments	14,000	
Total investments	$98,646	

	1993	
	Gross Unrealized Losses	Amortized Costs
Bonds:		
U.S. Treasury securities and obligations of		
U.S. Government Corporations and Agencies	$ 2	$15,209
Obligations of states & political subdivisions	166	3,088
Corporate securities	27	21,532
Mortgage-backed securities	9	1,925
	204	41,754
Common and preferred stocks	696	24,862
Mortgage loans (estimated fair value of $849)		
Policy and student loans (1)		
Real estate		
Investments		
Short-term investments		
Total investments		

	1992	
	Carrying Value	Gross Unrealized Gains
Bonds:		
U.S. Treasury securities and obligations of		
U.S. Government Corporations and Agencies	$12,854	$ 612
Obligations of states & political subdivisions	406	—
Corporate securities	15,746	438

	1992	
	Carrying Value	Gross Unrealized Gains
	29,006	1,050
Common and preferred stocks (cost: $19,888)	29,529	
Mortgage loans (estimated fair value of $2,792)	2,674	
Policy and student loans (1)	4,837	
Real estate	46	
Investments	66,092	
Short-term investments	42,091	
Total investments	$108,183	

	1992	
	Gross Unrealized Losses	Estimated Market Value
Bonds:		
U.S. Treasury securities and obligations of U.S. Government Corporations and Agencies	$ 12	$13,454
Obligations of states & political subdivisions	300	106
Corporate securities	129	16,055
	441	29,615
Common and preferred stocks (cost: $19,888)		29,529
Mortgage loans (estimated fair value of $2,792)		
Policy and student loans (1)		
Real estate		
Investments		
Short-term investments		
Total investments		

(1) It is not practicable to estimate these loans' fair value without incurring excessive costs; therefore, these loans are carried at their historical costs.

At the end of fiscal 1993, the Company adopted Statement of Financial Accounting Standards 115 ("SFAS 115"), Accounting for Certain Investments in Debt and Equity Securities. The effect of the adoption of SFAS 115 was to increase net unrealized investment gains by $1,253. Mortgage loans, policy and student loans and real estate continue to be carried at historical cost.

Effective December 31, 1993, all of the Company's debt and equity securities are considered as available for sale and are carried at market value. Prior thereto bonds were reported at amortized cost. Market values of investment securities have been determined in accordance with methods prescribed by the National Association of Insurance Commissioners ("NAIC"). Such values are determined by market quotations when available. The market value for certain municipal bonds is assumed to be equal to amortized cost where no market quotations exist. If a decline in the value of a common stock, preferred stock, or publicly traded bond below its cost or amortized cost is considered to be other than temporary, a realized loss is recorded to reduce the carrying value of the investment to its estimated net realizable value, which becomes the new cost basis. Bonds having an amortized cost of $9,321 and $9,220 were on deposit with insurance regulatory authorities at December 31, 1993 and December 31, 1992, respectively, in accordance with statutory requirements.

The amortized cost and carrying value of debt securities at December 31, 1993 by contractual maturity are shown below. Actual maturities may differ from contractual maturities because borrowers may have the right to call or prepay obligations with or without call or prepayment penalties.

	Amortized Cost	Carrying Value
Due in one year or less	$15,778	$15,783
Due after one year through five years	25,858	26,842
Due after five years through ten years	9,005	9,137
Due after ten years	3,004	3,172
Varying maturities	2,109	2,109
Totals	$55,754	$57,043

Investment income was earned from the following sources:

	1993	1992	1991
Bonds	$2,602	$2,244	$3,269
Common and preferred stocks	1,365	1,054	523
Mortgage loans	163	277	286
Other, primarily short-term investments	1,274	2,121	3,366
Total investment income	5,404	5,696	7,444
Less investment expenses	(345)	(330)	(265)
Net investment income	$5,059	$5,366	$7,179

The cost of securities sold is based on specific identification. Unrealized gains (losses) in the value of bonds and preferred and common stocks, net of related minority interests, are accounted for as a direct increase or decrease in shareholders' equity and, accordingly, have no effect on net income (loss).

A summary of realized investment gains (losses) follows:

	1993		
	Stocks	Bonds	Total
Gains	$1,231	$ 91	$1,322
Losses	(313)	(213)	(526)
Write-downs	(52)	—	(52)
Total realized investment gains (losses), net	$ 866	$(122)	$ 744

	1992		
	Stocks	Bonds	Total
Gains	$4,019	$ 310	$4,329
Losses	(131)	(107)	(238)
Total realized investment gains, net	$3,888	$ 203	$4,091

	1991			
	Stocks	Bonds	Real Estate	Total
Gains	$ 84	$ 59	$ 91	$ 234
Losses	(1)	(184)	—	(185)
Write-downs	(974)	(6,167)	—	(7,141)
Total realized investment gains (losses), net	$(891)	$(6,292)	$ 91	$(7,092)

Proceeds from the sale of equity and debt securities (excluding short-term investments) are as follows:

68

	1993	1992	1991
Equity Securities	$ 8,197	$ 9,298	$ 273
Debt Securities	1,218	10,250	6,313

Investments which exceed 10% of shareholders' equity at December 31, 1993 are as follows:

	Cost	Carrying Value
Bonds:		
Data South Computer	$3,000	$ 3,000
Sears	3,000	3,237
Xerox Corporation	2,995	3,230
Common Stock:		
Wachovia Corporation	3,527	11,654
Short-term investments:		
Ecolab, Inc.	4,000	4,000
Universal Corporation	3,000	3,000

The Company's bond portfolio consisted of a total of 99% investment grade securities at December 31, 1993 as defined by the NAIC.

FIRE, MARINE, OR CASUALTY INSURANCE COMPANIES

ALLCITY INSURANCE COMPANY, DECEMBER 31, 1993

Allcity Insurance Company
Consolidated Balance Sheets
(thousands of dollars, except share and per share amounts)

	December 31,	
	1993	1992
Assets		
Investments	$219,608	$ 199,220
. . . .		
Capital		
. . . .		
Net unrealized gain on investments (net of income taxes of $1,397)	2,581	
. . . .		

Allcity Insurance Company
Consolidated Statements of Income
(*thousands of dollars, except share and per share amounts*)

	Year Ended December 31,		
	1993	1992	1991
Revenues			
. . . .			
Net investment income	12,265	12,777	12,102
. . . .			
Net securities gains	1,413	1,551	297

Allcity Insurance Company
Consolidated Statements of Changes in Capital Accounts
(*in thousands*)

	Net Unrealized Gain/(Loss) on Investments
Balance at December 31, 1992	—
Cumulative effect of change in accounting principle	2,581
Balance at December 31, 1993	$2,581

Notes to Consolidated Financial Statements
Allcity Insurance Company

Note 2 — Accounting Policies

. . . .

Investments. In May 1993, the Financial Accounting Standards Board issued Statement No. 115 "Accounting for Certain Investments in Debt and Equity Securities" ("SFAS 115"). The Company adopted SFAS 115 on December 31, 1993. Under SFAS 115, marketable debt and equity securities are designated as either (1) "held to maturity" and carried at amortized cost, (2) "trading" and carried at fair value with differences between cost and fair value reflected in results of operations or (3) "available for sale" and carried at fair value with differences between cost and fair value being reflected as a separate component of shareholders' equity, net of income tax effect. The adoption of SFAS 115 resulted in an increase in capital of $2,581,000 (net of applicable income tax) at December 31, 1993. The company does not expect that SFAS 115 will have a material effect on future results of operations, although the Company believes it is likely to result in substantial fluctuations in capital.

At December 31, 1993, short-term investments (stated at cost) and investments in debt securities (stated at amortized cost) on deposit with the New York State Insurance Department, both of which the Company has the positive intent and ability to hold to maturity, are classified as "Investments held to maturity." All other investments in debt securities at that date are classified as "Investments available for sale" and stated at fair value. Net unrealized appreciation/(depreciation) on investments available for sale (net of tax) is included as a separate component in capital.

In 1992, fixed maturities (other than those classified as held for sale) are stated at amortized cost except where a nontemporary decline in market value is identified, in which case, market value is utilized. Net unrealized appreciation/(depreciation) on equity securities (none held at December 31,

1993 and 1992) is included in capital. At December 31, 1992, short-term investments are stated at cost which approximates market.

Investments classified as held for sale at December 31, 1992, which were sold in March 1993 to utilize the remaining capital loss carryforwards of Phlcorp, were carried at the lower of amortized cost or market value. Gains or losses incurred upon disposal of investments are determined on a specific identification basis and are included in net income.

. . . .

Note 4 — Investment Operations

Investment income is summarized as follows:

	Year Ended December 31,		
	1993	1992	1991
	(*thousands of dollars*)		
Investment income:			
Fixed maturities	$12,147	$11,244	$10,155
Short-term investments	372	899	1,117
Dividends	—	919	1,081
	12,519	13,062	12,353
Less: Investment expenses	254	285	251
Net Investment Income	$12,265	$12,777	$12,102

Investments at December 31, 1993 are summarized as follows:

	Amortized Cost	Gross Unrealized Gains	Gross Unrealized Losses
	(*thousands of dollars*)		
Investments Available for Sale:			
U.S. Treasury securities and obligations of U.S. government agencies	$144,121	$2,376	$263
Mortgage-backed securities	50,452	1,502	19
Foreign governments	100		7
Public utilities	2,305	139	
All other corporate bonds	15,140	255	5
Total Investments Available for Sale	212,118	4,272	294
Investments Held to Maturity:			
U.S. Treasury securities	480	57	
Short-term investments	3,032	—	—
Total Investments Held to Maturity	3,512	57	
Total Investments	$215,630	$4,329	$294

	Aggregate Fair Value	Carrying Amount
	(*thousands of dollars*)	
Investments Available for Sale:		
U.S. Treasury securities and obligations of U.S. government agencies	$ 146,234	$ 146,234

Note 4 — Investment Operations (continued)

	Aggregate Fair Value	Carrying Amount
	(thousands of dollars)	
Mortgage-backed securities	51,935	51,935
Foreign governments	93	93
Public utilities	2,444	2,444
All other corporate bonds	15,390	15,390
Total Investments Available for Sale	216,096	216,096
Investments Held to Maturity:		
U.S. Treasury securities	537	480
Short-term investments	3,032	3,032
Total Investments Held to Maturity	3,569	3,512
Total Investments	$219,665	$219,608

Investments at December 31, 1992 are summarized as follows:

	Amortized Cost	Gross Unrealized Gains	Gross Unrealized Losses
	(thousands of dollars)		
U.S. Treasury securities and obligations of U.S. government agencies	$ 82,310	$1,539	$643
Mortgage-backed securities	60,452	1,497	98
Foreign governments	100	—	7
Public utilities	2,912	34	16
All other corporate bonds	5,856	53	33
Investments held for sale	16,133	99	80
Short-term investments	31,457	—	—
Total Investments	$199,220	$3,222	$877

	Aggregate Market Value	Carrying Amount
	(thousands of dollars)	
U.S. Treasury securities and obligations of U.S. government agencies	$ 83,206	$ 82,310
Mortgage-backed securities	61,851	60,452
Foreign governments	93	100
Public utilities	2,930	2,912
All other corporate bonds	5,876	5,856
Investments held for sale	16,152	16,133
Short-term investments	31,457	31,457
Total Investments	$201,565	$199,220

The amortized cost of fair value of investments at December 31, 1993, by contractual maturity, is shown below:

	Amortized Costs	Aggregate Fair Value
	(thousands of dollars)	
Investments available for sale:		
Due in one year or less	$ 13,070	$ 13,249
Due after one year through five years	126,744	128,987
Due after five years through ten years	21,777	21,856
Due after ten years	75	69
Sub-total	161,666	164,161
Mortgage-backed securities	50,452	51,935
Sub-total	212,118	216,096
Investments held to maturity:		
Due in one year or less	3,032	3,032
Due after one year through five years	480	537
Total Investments	$215,630	$219,665

Expected maturities will differ from contractual maturities because borrowers may have the right to call or prepay obligations with or without call or prepayment penalties.

The Company sold certain of its investments in debt securities during 1993, 1992, and 1991. Gross gains of $1,413,000, $2,579,000 and $321,000 were realized on these sales in 1993, 1992, and 1991, respectively. Gross losses of $24,000 and $24,000 were realized on those sales in 1992 and 1991, respectively. A gross loss of $1,004,000 was realized on the sale of equity securities in 1992.

The changes in unrealized gains (losses) on investments in fixed maturities were $1,690,000, $(2,903,000) and $5,587,000 for the years ended December 31, 1993, 1992, and 1991, respectively. For the investment in equity securities, the changes in unrealized gains were $696,000 and $616,000 for the years ended December 31, 1992 and 1991, respectively. The Company sold its investment in equity securities in 1992.

ST. PAUL COMPANIES INC., DECEMBER 31, 1993

The St. Paul Companies
Consolidated Statements of Operations

	Year Ended December 31,		
(in thousands)	1993	1992	1991
. . . .			
Revenues			
. . . .			
Realized investment gains	58,254	57,451	38,008
. . . .			

The St. Paul Companies
Consolidated Balance Sheets

	December 31,	
(in thousands)	1993	1992

Consolidated Balance Sheets (continued)

(*in thousands*)	December 31,	
	1993	1992
Assets		
Investments:		
Fixed maturities	$ 9,147,964	$ 7,722,479
Equities	548,682	493,797
. . . .		
Investment banking inventory securities	305,804	226,332
. . . .		
Common Shareholders' Equity		
. . . .		
Unrealized appreciation of investments	588,844	63,669

. . . .

The St. Paul Companies
Consolidated Statements of Common Shareholders' Equity

(*in thousands*)	Year Ended December 31, 1993
Unrealized appreciation of investments, net of taxes:	
Beginning of year	63,669
Change due to adoption of SFAS No. 115	501,982
Other changes for the year	23,193
End of year	588,844

The St. Paul Companies
Notes to Consolidated Financial Statements

Note 1 — A Summary of Significant Accounting Policies

. . . .

Information About Our Investments

New Method for Valuing Investments — We implemented SFAS No. 115, "Accounting for Certain Investments in Debt and Equity Securities" as of Dec. 31, 1993. We classified our entire fixed maturity and equity investment portfolios as "available-for-sale." Accordingly, these investments are reported at estimated market value at Dec. 31, 1993, with unrealized gains and losses (net of deferred taxes) recorded in common shareholders' equity. Prior years' financial statements were not restated. Classifying these portfolios as "available-for-sale" did not impact net income.

Fixed Maturities — We carry our fixed maturities at estimated market value as of Dec. 31, 1993. Prior to our adoption of SFAS No. 115, we carried fixed maturities at amortized cost.

Equities — We carry our equity securities at estimated market value, consistent with prior years.

. . . .

Realized Investment Gains and Losses — We record the cost of each individual investment security so that when we sell, we are able to identify and record the gain or loss on that transaction.

We continually monitor the difference between the cost and estimated market value of our investments. If any of our investments experience a decline in value that is other than temporary, we establish a valuation allowance for the decline and record a realized loss on the statement of operations.

Unrealized Appreciation and Depreciation of Investments — For investments we carry at estimated market value, we record the difference between cost and market, net of deferred taxes, as a part of common shareholders' equity. This difference is referred to as unrealized appreciation or depreciation of investments.

. . . .

Note 3 — Investments

Valuation of Investments — The following presents the cost, gross unrealized appreciation and depreciation, and estimated market value of our investments in fixed maturities, equities and venture capital.

(in thousands)	Cost	December 31, 1993 Gross Unrealized Appreciation	Gross Unrealized Depreciation	Estimated Market Value
Fixed maturities:				
U.S. government	$1,854,287	$ 89,183	$ (4,478)	$1,938,992
States and political subdivisions	4,108,680	502,819	(581)	4,610,918
Foreign governments	520,254	47,515	(3,070)	564,699
Corporate securities	957,526	66,917	(8,369)	1,016,074
Mortgage-backed securities	944,352	74,361	(1,432)	1,017,281
Total fixed maturities	8,385,099	780,795	(17,930)	9,147,964
Equities	488,383	80,398	(20,099)	548,682
Venture capital	224,523	89,100	(15,641)	297,982
Total	$9,098,005	$950,293	$(53,670)	$9,994,628

(in thousands)	Cost	December 31, 1992 Gross Unrealized Appreciation	Gross Unrealized Depreciation	Estimated Market Value
Fixed maturities:				
U.S. government	$1,322,264	$ 70,779	$ (88)	$1,392,955
States and political subdivisions	4,248,793	311,687	(2,758)	4,557,722
Foreign governments	391,598	22,066	(625)	413,039
Corporate securities	564,584	10,840	(11,106)	564,318
Mortgage-backed securities	1,203,972	104,916	(620)	1,308,268
Total fixed maturities	7,731,211	520,288	(15,197)	8,236,302
Equities	409,505	94,553	(10,261)	493,797
Venture capital	210,250	33,469	(12,560)	231,159
Total	$8,350,966	$648,310	$(38,018)	$8,961,258

. . . .

Fixed Maturities by Maturity Date — Presented below is a breakdown of our fixed maturities by years to maturity. Actual maturities may differ from those stated as a result of calls and prepayments.

(in thousands)	December 31, 1993	
	Amortized Cost	Estimated Market Value
One year or less	$ 114,598	$ 115,325
Over one year through five years	758,056	804,925
Over five years through ten years	2,133,120	2,311,488
Over ten years	4,434,973	4,898,945
Mortgage-backed securities with various maturities	944,352	1,017,281
Total	$8,385,099	$9,147,964

Note 4 — Investment Transactions

Investment Activity — Here is a summary of our investment purchases, sales and maturities.

(in thousands)	Year Ended December 31,		
	1993	1992	1991
Purchases			
Fixed maturities	$1,816,965	$1,778,736	$1,671,570
Equities	465,056	401,374	397,164
Real estate	110,371	64,658	46,298
Venture capital	79,410	55,928	50,558
Other investments	12,929	15,176	35,625
Total purchases	2,484,731	2,315,872	2,201,215

(in thousands)	Year Ended December 31,		
	1993	1992	1991
Proceeds from Sales and Maturities			
Fixed maturities:			
Sales	169,330	295,648	361,734
Maturities and redemptions	1,236,912	976,712	601,448
Equities	437,610	431,225	464,145
Real estate	40,764	—	31,248
Venture capital	59,124	2,803	15,926
Other investments	10,466	15,110	32,412
Total sales and maturities	1,954,206	1,721,498	1,506,913
Net purchases	$530,525	$594,374	$694,302

Net Investment Income — Here is a summary of our net investment income.

(in thousands)	Year Ended December 31,		
	1993	1992	1991
Fixed maturities	$607,067	$605,217	$589,048

(in thousands)	Year Ended December 31,		
	1993	1992	1991
Equities	12,035	11,629	12,763
Real estate	19,288	19,022	15,298
Venture capital	(2,012)	(1,966)	(1,156)
Other investments	698	569	5,353
Short-term investments	37,952	46,018	67,622
Total	675,028	680,489	688,928
Investment expenses	(13,922)	(14,115)	(13,324)
Net investment income	$661,106	$666,374	$675,604

Realized and Unrealized Investment Gains (Losses) — The following summarizes our pretax realized investment gains and losses and change in pretax unrealized appreciation.

(in thousands)	Year Ended December 31,		
	1993	1992	1991
Pretax Realized Investment Gains (Losses)			
Fixed maturities:			
Gross realized gains	$ 8,916	$ 12,702	$ 6,488
Gross realized losses	(3,585)	(1,391)	(2,209)
Total fixed maturities	5,331	11,311	4,279
Equities:			
Gross realized gains	62,310	81,841	80,658
Gross realized losses	(18,782)	(16,066)	(20,048)
Total equities	43,528	65,775	60,610
Real estate	(10,188)	(7,519)	(644)
Venture capital	24,046	(180)	(4,167)
Other	(4,463)	11,936)	(22,070)
Total pretax realized investment gains	$58,254	$57,451	$38,008

(in thousands)	Year Ended December 31,		
	1993	1992	1991
Change in Pretax Unrealized Appreciation			
Fixed maturities	$257,774	$ 13,297	$317,542
Equities	(23,993)	(34,038)	65,343
Venture capital	52,550	6,687	15,962
Total change in pretax unrealized appreciation	$286,331	$(14,054)	$398,847

IV

NONFINANCIAL ENTERPRISES

Enterprises that do not provide financial services usually have fewer investments in debt and equity securities to be accounted for in accordance with FASB Statement No. 115 than enterprises that provide financial services. Examples of accounting for such investments in accordance with FASB Statement No. 115 by twenty-two enterprises that operate primarily in fields other than the provision of financial services are presented below. The examples are classified according to whether the reporting enterprise owns trading securities.

NO TRADING SECURITIES OWNED

ARMCO INC., DECEMBER 31, 1993

Statement of Consolidated Operations
For the Years Ended December 31, 1993, 1992, and 1991
(dollars in millions, except per share amounts)

	1993	1992	1991
. . . .			
Sundry other — net	(36.1)	(5.5)	(20.9)
. . . .			

Notes to Financial Statements
(dollar amounts in millions, except per share amounts)

1 — Summary of Accounting Policies

. . . .

Investments

. . . .

In 1993, Armco adopted Statement of Financial Accounting Standards (SFAS) 115, Accounting for Certain Investments in Debt and Equity Securities, which provides guidance as to when it is appropriate to report certain invested assets at fair market value. Under the definitions provided in this Statement at December 31, 1993, Armco's invested assets, totaling $203.0, have been classified as held to maturity and are therefore properly recorded at amortized cost. There was no material effect to Armco as a result of adopting this standard.

. . . .

Sales of marketable securities and other cost investments resulted in gains of $14.1 in 1991, which are reported in Sundry other — net.

ATRIX LABORATORIES INC., SEPTEMBER 30, 1993

Atrix Laboratories, Inc.
Balance Sheets

	September 30	
	1993	1992
Current Assets:		
. . . .		
Marketable securities, at cost (Note 2)	—	7,088,813
Marketable securities available-for-sale (Note 2)	8,369,435	7,029,927
. . . .		
Total current assets	10,327,525	18,764,836
Marketable Securities, at Cost (Note 2)	17,446,683	16,573,781
. . . .		
Shareholders' Equity:		
. . . .		
Unrealized holding gain on securities available-for-sale (Note 2)	59,634	—
. . . .		

Atrix Laboratories Inc.
Statements of Operations

	For the Years Ended September 30,		
	1993	1992	1991

Revenue:

. . . .

Gain on sale of securities	157,681	—	—

. . . .

Atrix Laboratories, Inc.
Statements of Changes in Shareholders' Equity

	Unrealized Holding Gain
Balance, September 30, 1992	—
Unrealized holding gain	59,634
Balance, September 30, 1993	$59,634

Atrix Laboratories, Inc. Financial Report
Notes to the Financial Statements

1. Organization and Summary of Significant Accounting Policies

. . . .

Investments. Investments in marketable securities are stated at the amortized cost at the balance sheet date. The Company has the ability and intent to hold such securities to maturity. Premiums and discounts associated with bonds are amortized using the effective interest rate method. At September 30, 1993, securities available-for-sale are carried at fair value with the unrealized holding gain or loss included in shareholders' equity; at September 30, 1992, such securities were carried at the lower of cost or market.

. . . .

2. Marketable Securities

At September 30, 1993, the balances of current and non-current portfolios of marketable securities were as follows:

	Number of Shares Principal Amounts ($)	Cost	Fair Value
U.S. Government and Agency Bonds Funds — available-for-sale — current:			
Thornburg Fund	411,787	$5,288,713	$5,320,292
Thomson Fund	314,021	3,021,088	3,049,143
Total	725,808	$8,309,801	$8,369,435

2. Marketable Securities (continued)

	Number of Shares Principal Amounts ($)	Cost	Fair Value
U.S. Government and Agency Bonds — non-current	$16,595,000	$17,446,683	$17,889,375

The U.S. Government and Agency bonds mature in 1–5 years.

At September 30, 1992, the balances of current and non-current portfolios of marketable securities were as follows:

	Number of Shares Principal Amounts ($)	Cost	Fair Value
U.S. Government and Agency Bonds — current	$ 7,000,000	$ 7,088,813	$ 7,112,186
U.S. Government and Agency Bonds — held for sale — current	$ 7,000,000	$ 7,029,927	$ 7,172,200
U.S. Government and Agency Bonds — non-current	$16,000,000	$16,573,781	$17,134,063

The Company has adopted Statement of Financial Accounting Standards No. 115 "Accounting for Certain Investments in Debt and Equity Securities" as of September 30, 1993. This statement requires that marketable securities that are available-for-sale be stated at fair value with the difference between cost and fair value included as a component of shareholders' equity.

At September 30, 1993, the gross unrealized gains and gross unrealized losses pertaining to marketable securities were as follows:

	Gains	Losses
Held-to-maturity — non-current	$446,785	$4,093
Available-for-sale	59,634	—
Total unrealized gains/losses	$506,419	$4,093

For the years ended September 30, 1993, the proceeds from the sale of marketable securities available-for-sale and the resulting gain or loss were:

	Proceeds	Gain/(Loss)
Total Gain	$ 7,294,020	$129,007
Total Loss	4,020,100	(12,643)
Total	$11,314,120	$116,364

CFW COMMUNICATIONS COMPANY, DECEMBER 31, 1993

CFW Communications Company and Subsidiaries
Consolidated Balance Sheets

	1993	1992	1991

Assets

. . . .

	1993	1992	1991
Securities and Investments (Note 2)	31,250,914	7,538,798	6,909,435

. . . .

Shareholders' Equity

. . . .

| Unrealized gain on securities held for sale, net | 13,737,504 | — | — |

. . . .

CFW Communications Company and Subsidiaries
Notes to Consolidated Financial Statements

Note 1. Significant Accounting Policies

. . . .

Securities and Investments. During 1993 the Company adopted Statement of Financial Accounting Standards No. 115, "Accounting for Certain Investments in Debt and Equity Securities."

Securities classified as available for sale are those the Company intends to hold for an indefinite period of time. Any decision to sell a security classified as available for sale would be based on various factors, including significant movements in market value, liquidity needs and other similar factors. Securities available for sale are carried at fair value. Unrealized gains and losses are reported as increases or decreases in shareholders' equity, net of the related deferred tax effect. Realized gains and losses, determined on the basis of the cost of specific securities sold, are included in earnings.

. . . .

Market values are not available for most of the Company's investments. Information regarding each investment is reviewed continuously for evidence of impairment in value. No impairment was deemed to have occurred at December 31, 1993.

. . . .

Note 2. Securities and Investments

Investments consist of the following:

Available for Sale	Type of Ownership	Carrying Values		
		1993	1992	1991
American Telecasting Inc.	Equity Securities	$25,983,612	$3,499,972	$3,499,972
(including unrealized gain of $ 22,483,640 in 1993)				

. . . .

Note 2. Securities and Investments (continued)

Available for Sale	Type of Ownership	Carrying Values		
		1993	1992	1991
Cost Method				
Independent Telecommunications Network, Inc.	Equity and Convertible Debt Securities	1,677,200	1,677,200	1,677,200
American Quality (See Note 9)	Equity Securities	534,589	—	—
Other	Equity Securities	216,914	345,251	123,500
		2,428,703	2,022,451	1,800,700
		$31,250,914	$7,538,798	$6,909,435

Note 9. Commitments

. . . .

Subsequent to December 31, 1993, the Company acquired for cash in a purchase transaction, all of the outstanding stock of American Quality Cable (AQC) for approximately $13,400,000. In connection with the purchase, the Company also retired $2,900,000 of AQC's outstanding debt.

. . . .

CONTINENTAL MEDICAL SYSTEMS INC., JUNE 30, 1993

Continental Medical Systems, Inc. and Subsidiaries
Consolidated Statements of Income

	Years Ended June 30,		
	1993	1992	1991
	(in thousands, except share data)		

. . . .

Income before cumulative effect of accounting change	22,723	27,091	18,501
Cumulative effect of accounting change (Note 11)	(3,204)	—	—
Net income	$19,519	$27,091	$18,501

Continental Medical Systems, Inc. and Subsidiaries
Notes to Consolidated Financial Statements
Years Ended June 30, 1993, 1992, and 1991

11. Adoption of New Accounting Principle

In fiscal 1993, the Company adopted the provisions of Statement of Financial Accounting Standards No. 115, "Accounting for Certain Investments in Debt and Equity Securities." In applying this statement, the Company recognized a $5,000,000 write-down to fair value of a long-term care investment being held to maturity. The cumulative effect of this change in accounting principle, on an after-tax basis, was $3,204,000 or $.08 per share on a fully diluted basis.

FISERV INC., DECEMBER 31, 1993

Fiserv Inc.
Consolidated Balance Sheets

	December 31,	
	1993	1992
Assets		
. . . .		
Investment securities (Note 1)	661,309,000	589,702,000
Other investments (Note 1)	34,831,000	17,447,000
. . . .		
Shareholders' equity:		
. . . .		
Unrealized gain on investments	9,230,000	
. . . .		

Fiserv Inc.
Consolidated Statements of Changes in Shareholders' Equity

	Year Ended December 31,		
	1993	1992	1991
Unrealized gain on investments	9,230,000		

Fiserv Inc.
Notes to Consolidated Financial Statements
For the Years Ended December 31, 1993, 1992, and 1991

Note 1 — Summary of Significant Accounting Policies

. . . .

Trust Account Deposits and Investment Securities. The Company's trust administration subsidiary accepts money market deposits from its trust customers and invests the funds in securities. Such amounts due trust depositors represent the primary source of funds for the Company's investment securities and amounted to $663,426,000 and $589,778,000 in 1993 and 1992, respectively. The related investment securities comprised the following at December 31, 1993 and 1992:

1993	Principal Amount	Cost	Market Value
U.S. Government and government agency obligations	$357,975,000	$363,406,000	$364,778,000
Corporate bonds	36,975,000	37,390,000	37,253,000
Repurchase agreements	179,942,000	179,942,000	179,942,000
Federal funds sold	10,500,000	10,500,000	10,500,000
Asset backed securities	48,025,000	48,062,000	48,158,000
Medium term notes	33,500,000	33,349,000	33,563,000
Money market funds	24,200,000	24,207,000	24,199,000
Premium amortization, etc.		(863,000)	33,000
Total	$691,117,000	695,993,000	$698,426,000

Included in:

Cash and cash equivalents	20,904,000	
Other investments	13,780,000	
Trust account investments	$661,309,000	

1992	Principal Amount	Cost	Market Value
U.S. Government and government agency obligations	$276,012,000	$279,944,000	$280,612,000
Corporate bonds	43,500,000	43,779,000	43,817,000
Repurchase agreements	30,139,000	30,139,000	30,139,000
Commercial paper	116,500,000	115,356,000	115,888,000
Certificates of deposit	5,000,000	4,996,000	5,019,000
Asset backed securities	56,339,000	56,960,000	56,722,000
Medium term notes	68,295,000	68,429,000	68,650,000
Money market funds	21,500,000	21,500,000	21,500,000
Accrued interest, premium amortization, etc.		2,138,000	2,989,000
Total	$617,285,000	$623,241,000	$625,336,000

Included in:

Cash and cash equivalents	26,889,000	
Other investments	6,650,000	
Trust account investments	$589,702,000	

Substantially all of the investments have contractual maturities of one year or less except for government agency obligations which generally contain provisions for interest rate resets.

During 1993, the Company recorded in shareholders' equity an unrealized gain, net of income taxes, on its investment in The BISYS Group, Inc. in accordance with the provisions of Financial Accounting Standards No. 115, Accounting for Certain Investments in Debt and Equity Securities.

FLORIDA EAST COAST INDUSTRIES INC., DECEMBER 31, 1993

Consolidated Balance Sheets
December 31, 1993 and 1992
(dollars in thousands except per share amounts)

	1993	1992
Assets		
Current Assets		
. . . .		
Short-term investments (Note 5)	18,009	18,797
. . . .		
Total current assets	78,976	77,478
Other Investments (Note 5)	66,233	78,545
. . . .		
Shareholders' Equity		
. . . .		
Net unrealized gain on debt and marketable equity securities (Note 5)	891	—
. . . .		

Notes to Consolidated Financial Statements
December 31, 1993, 1992, 1991

3. Summary of Significant Accounting Policies

. . . .

Investments. Investments consist principally of municipal bonds, common stocks, redeemable preferred stocks, and U.S. Government obligations. The Company adopted the provisions of Statement of Financial Accounting Standards No. 115, "Accounting for Certain Investments in Debt and Equity Securities" as of December 31, 1993. Under Statement 115, the Company classifies its debt and marketable equity securities in one of three categories: trading, available-for-sale or held-to-maturity. Trading securities are bought and held principally for the purpose of selling them in the near-term. Held-to-maturity securities are those securities which the Company has the ability and intent to hold until maturity. All other securities not included in trading or held-to-maturity are classified as available-for-sale.

Trading and available-for-sale securities are recorded at fair value. Held-to-maturity securities are recorded at amortized cost, adjusted for the amortization or accretion of premiums or discounts. Unrealized holding gains and losses on trading securities are included in earnings. Unrealized holding gains and losses, net of the related tax effect, on available-for-sale securities are excluded from earnings and are reported as a separate component of shareholders' equity until realized.

A decline in the market value of any available-for-sale or held-to-maturity security below cost that is deemed other than temporary is charged to earnings resulting in the establishment of a new cost basis for the security.

Realized gains and losses for securities classified as available-for-sale and held-to-maturity are included in earnings and are derived using the specific identification method for determining the cost of securities sold.

5. Investments

As discussed in Note 3, the Company adopted Statement 115 as of December 31, 1993. The cumulative effect of this change in accounting for investments of $1,451,000 is determined as of December 31, 1993 and is reported separately as a component of shareholders' equity net of related tax of $560,000. Investments at December 31, 1993 consist of (*in thousands*):

Short-term investments:

Held-to-maturity, at amortized cost	$18,009

Other investments:

Held-to-maturity, at amortized cost	$25,644
Available for sale, at fair value	40,589
Total other investments	$66,233

Other investments, including certain held-to-maturity investments which mature within one year, are held as a development fund created to accumulate capital expected to be required for future improvement of the Company's real estate properties. The amortized cost and fair value for available-for-sale and held-to-maturity securities by major security type at December 31, 1993, were as follows:

	Amortized Cost	Fair Value	Net Unrealized Holding Gain (Loss)
Available-for-Sale:			
Municipal Bonds (*)	$29,961	$31,387	$1,426
Equity Securities	9,177	9,202	25
Total	$39,138	$40,589	$1,451
Held-to-Maturity:			
Certificates of Deposit (**)	$ 2,259	$ 2,259	$ —
Mortgage Backed Securities (*)	916	1,491	575
Municipal Bonds (*)	2,401	2,376	(25)
Corporate Debt Securities (*)	801	801	—
U.S. Treasury Securities (**)	37,276	38,500	1,224
Total	$43,653	$45,427	$1,774

(*) Due principally after five years.
(**) Due within one year.

Gross unrealized holding gains and gross unrealized holding losses at December 31, 1993 were $3,667,000 and $442,000, respectively. At December 31, 1992, investments are carried at amortized cost ($97,342,000) which approximates quoted market prices ($99,148,000).

IMPERIAL HOLLY CORP., MARCH 31, 1994

Imperial Holly Corporation and Subsidiaries
Consolidated Balance Sheets

	March 31,	
	1994	1993
	(in thousands of dollars)	
Assets		
Current Assets:		
Cash and temporary investments	$ 555	$ 9,405
Marketable securities (Note 2)	28,334	22,148
. . . .		
Total current assets	235,651	232,385
Other Investments — at cost	6,553	6,799
. . . .		
Shareholders' Equity		
. . . .		
Unrealized securities gains — net of income taxes (Note 2)	3,804	—
. . . .		

Imperial Holly Corporation and Subsidiaries
Consolidated Statements of Income

	Year Ended March 31,		
	1994	1993	1992
		(in thousands of dollars)	
. . . .			
Realized Securities Gains — Net (Note 2)	1,465	898	67
. . . .			

Imperial Holly Corporation and Subsidiaries
Consolidated Statements of Changes in Shareholders' Equity
(in thousands of dollars)

	Unrealized Securities Gains
Balance, March 31, 1993	—
Unrealized securities gains — net	$3,804
Balance, March 31, 1994	$3,804

2. Marketable Securities

Effective March 31, 1994, the Company adopted Statement of Financial Accounting Standards No. 115, Accounting for Certain Investments in Debt and Equity Securities ('SFAS No. 115'). All of the Company's marketable securities are classified as 'available for sale,' and accordingly, are reflected in the March 31, 1994 Consolidated Balance Sheet at fair market value, with the aggregate unrealized gain, net of related deferred tax liability, included in shareholders' equity. SFAS No. 115 may not be applied to prior periods, therefore the Company's marketable securities portfolio at March 31, 1993 is reported in the Consolidated Balance Sheet at amortized cost. Adoption of SFAS No. 115 had no effect on reported earnings. Cost for determining gains and losses on sales of marketable securities is determined on the FIFO method. Marketable securities consisted of the following (*in thousands of dollars*):

				March 31, 1994	
			Fair	Gross	
		Amortized	Market	Unrealized	Holding
	Shares	Cost	Value	Gains	Losses
US Government securities					
due 1995 through 1997		$ 1,295	$ 1,308	$ 22	$ (9)
Municipal securities due 1996		1,482	1,472	—	(10)
Corporate debt securities					
due 2015		1,093	1,104	11	—
Preferred stocks		698	981	283	—
Common stocks:					
Philip Morris Companies Inc.	142,700	4,036	7,224	3,188	—
Food and beverage stocks		4,480	6,732	2,320	(68)
Health care stocks		2,787	2,400	30	(417)
Energy stocks		1,984	2,267	289	(6)
Other common stocks		4,626	4,846	407	(187)
Total common stocks		17,913	23,469	6,234	(678)
Total		$22,481	$28,334	$6,550	$(697)

				March 31, 1993	
			Fair	Gross	
		Amortized	Market	Unrealized	Holding
	Shares	Cost	Value	Gains	Losses
US Government securities		$ 1,736	$ 1,875	$ 139	—
Municipal securities		2,376	2,401	25	—
Preferred stocks		2,015	2,571	556	—
Common stocks:					
Philip Morris Companies Inc.	175,000	4,816	11,200	6,384	—
Food and beverage stocks		4,480	7,580	3,113	$ (13)
Health care stocks		2,787	2,778	189	(198)
Energy stocks		1,454	1,693	239	—
Other common stocks		2,484	2,898	419	(5)
Total common stocks		16,021	26,149	10,344	(216)
Total		$22,148	$32,996	$11,064	$(216)

Realized securities gains are reported net of realized losses of $0 in 1994, $49,000 in 1993 and $19,000 in 1992. Marketable securities with a market value of $5,527,000 at March 31, 1994 were pledged to secure certain insurance obligations.

KAISER RESOURCES INC., DECEMBER 31, 1993

Kaiser Resources Inc. and Subsidiaries
Consolidated Balance Sheet

	December 31, 1993	December 31, 1992
. . . .		
Current Assets		
. . . .		
Short-term investments (Note 3)	10,041,619	—
. . . .		

Kaiser Steel Resources, Inc. and Subsidiaries
Notes to Consolidated Financial Statements

Note 3. Accounting Changes

Effective December 31, 1993, the Company adopted the Financial Accounting Standards Board issued Statement of Financial Accounting Standards ("SFAS") No. 115, "Accounting for Certain Investments in Debt and Equity Securities." SFAS No. 115 mandates that a determination be made of the appropriate classification for debt securities at the time of purchase and a reevaluation of such designation as of each balance sheet date. At December 31, 1993, short-term investments include treasury bills and certificates of deposit with maturities within one year which management classifies as "held to maturity." These debt securities are carried on the balance sheet at the lower cost or market. As cost approximates market, there are no unrealized gains or losses. The effect of the adoption of SFAS No. 115 is immaterial.

QUEST MEDICAL INC., DECEMBER 31, 1993

Quest Medical Inc.
Consolidated Balance Sheets

	December 31,	
	1993	1992
Assets		
Current Assets:		
. . . .		
Marketable securities	5,999,701	6,526,306
. . . .		

Consolidated Balance Sheets (continued)

| | December 31, | |
	1993	1992
Stockholders' Equity:		
. . . .		
Unrealized loss on marketable securities	(169,308)	—

. . . .

Quest Medical Inc.
Consolidated Statements of Earnings

| | For the Years Ended December 31, | | |
	1993	1992	1991
. . . .			
Other Income (Expense):			
Gain on sale of marketable securities	462,178	136,840	170,345
Unrealized loss on marketable securities	(169,308)	—	(667,550)

. . . .

Quest Medical Inc.
Consolidated Statements of Stockholders' Equity

	Unrealized Loss on Marketable Securities
Balance at December 31, 1992	—
Adjustment to unrealized losses on marketable securities	(169,308)
Balance at December 31, 1993	(169,308)

Quest Medical Inc.
Notes to Consolidated Financial Statements
The Years Ended December 31, 1993, 1992, and 1991

(1) Summary of Significant Accounting Policies

. . . .

(c) Marketable Securities

Effective December 31, 1993, the Company's marketable equity securities and debt securities are classified as available-for-sale. Available-for-sale securities are carried at fair value, with the unrealized gains and losses, net of tax, reported in a separate component of shareholders' equity. The amortized cost of debt securities in this category is adjusted for amortization of premiums and accretion of discounts to maturity. Such amortization is included in investment income. Realized gains and losses and declines in value judged to be other-than-temporary are included in other income. The cost of securities sold is based on the specific identification method. Interest and dividends on securities classified as available-for-sale are included in investment income. Prior to December 31, 1993, marketable securities were accounted for at the lower of cost or market.

The following is a summary of available-for-sale securities at December 31, 1993:

	Cost	Gross Unrealized Gains	Gross Unrealized Losses	Estimated Fair Value
Investment grade preferred securities	$2,922,046	4,500	55,259	2,871,287
Government-backed securities	255,000	—	4,387	250,613
Tax-free mutual funds	300,000	—	7,500	292,500
Real estate investment trusts	2,066,624	7,883	59,695	2,014,812
Other	625,339	37,190	92,040	570,489
	$6,169,009	49,573	218,881	5,999,701

Marketable securities at December 31, 1992 are stated at cost which approximated market and consisted of the following:

	1992
Mutual funds	$1,080,000
Government-backed securities	3,211,243
Investment-grade preferred securities	2,235,063
	$6,526,306

. . . .

(j) Accounting Changes

In May 1993, the Financial Accounting Standards Board issued Statement of Financial Accounting Standards No. 115, "Accounting for Certain Investments in Debt and Equity Securities." As permitted under the Statement, the Company has elected to adopt the provisions of the new standard as of the end of its current fiscal year. In accordance with the Statement, prior period financial statements have not been restated to reflect the change in accounting principle. The cumulative effect as of December 31, 1993 of adopting Statement 115, including the reversal of unrealized losses recorded in the current year, increased net income by $169,308. The ending balance of stockholders' equity was decreased by $169,308 to reflect the net unrealized holding loss on securities classified as available-for-sale.

SJW CORPORATION, DECEMBER 31, 1993

SJW Corp. and Subsidiaries
Consolidated Balance Sheet
The Years Ended December 31
(in thousands, except share data)

	1993	1992

° . . .

Other assets:		
Investment in California Water Service Company	21,999	13,090

Consolidated Balance Sheet (continued)
(in thousands)

	1993	1992

. . . .

Common shareholders' equity:

. . . .

Unrealized gain on investment	2,271	—

. . . .

SJW Corp. and Subsidiaries
Consolidated Statement of Changes
in Common Shareholders' Equity

	Unrealized Gain On Investment
Balances, December 31, 1992	—
Implementation of change in accounting for investment, net of tax effect of $1,579	2,271
Balances, December 31, 1993	2,271

SJW Corp. and Subsidiaries
Notes to Consolidated Financial Statements
(dollars in thousands, except share data)

Note 1. Summary of Significant Accounting Policies

. . . .

Investment in California Water Service Company. The Company adopted Statement of Financial Accounting Standards No. 115, "Accounting for Certain Investments in Debt and Equity Securities" effective December 31, 1993. Under this statement the Company's investment in California Water Service Company is reported at quoted market price, with the unrealized gain excluded from earnings and reported as a separate component of shareholders' equity. The adoption of Statement No. 115 resulted in increases in: investment in California Water Service Company, $3,850; deferred income taxes, $1,579; and common shareholders' equity, $2,271. At December 31, 1992, the Company's investment in California Water Service Company was reported at cost.

. . . .

SPRINT CORPORATION, DECEMBER 31, 1993

Consolidated Balance Sheets
As of December 31,
(in millions)

	1993	1992

. . . .

94

	1993	1992
Current assets		
. . . .		
Investment in common stock	130.2	—
. . . .		
Total current assets	1,977.9	1,664.0
Investments in common stocks	173.1	209.0
. . . .		
Common stock and other shareholders' equity		
. . . .		
Other	48.2	(44.7)
. . . .		

Notes to Consolidated Financial Statements

1. Accounting Policies

Investments in Common Stocks. Effective December 31, 1993, Sprint changed its method of accounting for its portfolio of marketable equity securities by adopting SFAS No. 115, "Accounting for Certain Investments in Debt and Equity Securities." Accordingly, such investments in common stocks are classified as available for sale and reported at fair value (estimated based on quoted market prices) as of December 31, 1993, and at cost as of December 31, 1992. As of December 31, 1993, the cost of such investments is $202 million, with the gross unrealized holding gains of $101 million reflected as an addition to other shareholders' equity, net of related income taxes. As of December 31, 1992, the market value of such investments was $278 million.

TELLABS INC., DECEMBER 31, 1993

Consolidated Balance Sheets
(in thousands)

	December 31, 1993	January 1, 1993
. . . .		
Stockholders' Equity		
. . . .		
Unrealized net holding gains on available-for-sale securities	28	—
. . . .		

Consolidated Balance Sheets (in thousands) (continued)

Consolidated Statements of Stockholders' Equity

(in thousands)	Unrealized Net Holding Gains
Balance at January 1, 1993	—
Unrealized net holding gains on available-for-sale securities	28
Balance at December 31, 1993	$ 28

Notes to Consolidated Financial Statements

Note B: Investments in Marketable Securities

As of December 31, 1993, the Company adopted a new accounting method for investment securities in accordance with Statement of Financial Accounting Standards No. 115. This standard requires the Company to designate its securities as held to maturity, available for sale, or trading. Securities held to maturity are accounted for at amortized cost, and management must express a positive intent to hold these securities to maturity. Available-for-sale securities are those that management designates as available to be sold in response to changes in market interest rates or liquidity needs. The Company does not invest in trading securities. The effect of this accounting change is applied prospectively; therefore, there is no restatement of prior-year investments or cumulative effect of a change in accounting principle for prior-year income.

Available-for-sale securities are accounted for at market with the unrealized gain or loss shown as a separate component of stockholders' equity. At December 31, 1993, they consisted of the following:

(in thousands)	Amortized Cost	Unrealized Gain (Loss)	Market Value
State and municipal securities	$8,073	$ (6)	$ 8,067
Preferred and common stocks	3,049	151	3,200
U.S. government and corporate debt obligations	4,832	(117)	4,715
	$15,954	$28	$15,982

Held-to-maturity securities are carried at their amortized cost. At December 31, 1993, the balance was $2,300,000, which consists entirely of certificates of deposit and corporate debt obligations. This amount is included in "Other Assets."

Investments in marketable securities carried at amortized cost at January 1, 1993, consisted of the following:

(in thousands)	
State and municipal securities	$21,919
Preferred stocks	7,307
Other marketable securities	9,888

TODD SHIPYARDS CORP., APRIL 3, 1994

Todd Shipyards Corporation
Consolidated Balance Sheets
April 3, 1994 and March 28, 1993
(in thousands of dollars)

	1994	1993
Assets:		
. . . .		
Securities available for sale	48,480	29,081
. . . .		

Todd Shipyards Corporation
Notes to Consolidated Financial Statements
April 3, 1994, March 28, 1993, and March 29, 1992

1. Principal Accounting Policies

. . . .

(G) Securities Available for Sale — The Company considers all debt instruments purchased with a maturity of more than three months to be securities available for sale. Securities available for sale consist primarily of U.S. Government securities and investment grade commercial paper.

On April 3, 1994, the Company adopted Statement of Financial Accounting Standards No. 115 "Accounting for Certain Investments in Debt and Equity Securities." In accordance with Statement 115, Company management determines the appropriate classification of debt securities at the time of purchase and reevaluates such designation as of each balance sheet date. Debt securities are classified as held-to-maturity when the Company has the positive intent and ability to hold the securities to maturity. Marketable equity and debt securities not held as trading assets in anticipation of short-term market movements and not classified as held-to-maturity are classified as available-for-sale.

Available-for-sale securities are carried at fair value, with the unrealized gains and losses, net of tax, reported in a separate component of shareholder's equity. The amortized cost of debt securities in this category is adjusted for amortization of premiums and accretion of discounts. Such amortization is included in investment income. Realized gains and losses and declines in value judged to be other-than-temporary are calculated based upon the amortized cost of the instrument and are included in investment income. The cost of securities sold is based on the specific identification method. Interest and dividends on available-for-sale securities are included in investment income.

3. Securities Available for Sale

The Company implemented Financial Accounting Standard No. 115 "Accounting for Certain Investments in Debt and Equity Securities" on April 3, 1994. The following is a summary of available-for-sale securities as of April 3, 1994:

(in thousands)	Cost	Gross Unrealized Gains	Gross Unrealized Losses	Estimated Fair Value
U.S. Treasury securities and agency obligations	$24,435	$ —	$145	$24,290
U.S. corporate securities	3,027	—	45	2,982
Mortgage-backed securities	21,653	6	451	21,208
	$49,115	$ 6	$641	$48,480

Gross realized gains on sales of available-for-sale securities totaled $19 thousand for the fiscal year ending April 3, 1994. The Company had no realized losses on sales of available-for-sale securities in fiscal year 1994.

The amortized cost and estimated fair value of the Company's available-for-sale debt and mortgage-backed securities at April 3, 1994, by contractual maturity, are shown below:

(in thousands)	Cost	Estimated Fair Value
Due in one year or less	$5,037	$5,026
Due after one year through three years	22,425	22,246
	27,462	27,272
Mortgage-backed securities	21,653	21,208
	$49,115	$48,480

TRANSTECHNOLOGY CORP., MARCH 31, 1994

Transtechnology Corp.
Statements of Consolidated Stockholders' Equity
For the Years Ended March 31, 1994, 1993, and 1992

	Other Stockholders' Equity
Balance, March 31, 1993	10,000
. . . .	
Unrealized investment holding losses	(1,569,000)
Balance, March 31, 1994	$(1,568,000)

TransTechnology Corporation and Subsidiaries
Notes to Consolidated Financial Statements

1. Summary of Accounting Principles

. . . .

Investments

On March 1, 1994, the Company acquired 365,000 shares of Mace Security International common stock, valued at $3.4 million, as partial payment for the sale of a division. At March 31, 1994, the Company adopted Statement of Financial Accounting Standards No. 115 "Accounting for Certain Investments in Debt and Equity Securities." The adoption of this statement resulted in a gross unrealized holding loss of $1.6 million, reported as a reduction to stockholders' equity in the March 31, 1994 Balance Sheet. The aggregate fair market value of the investment at March 31, 1994, was $1.8 million.

. . . .

XYLOGICS INC., OCTOBER 31, 1993

Xylogics Inc.
Notes to Consolidated Financial Statements

Note 1. Operations and Significant Accounting Policies

. . . .

In May 1993, the Financial Accounting Standards Board issued Statement of Financial Accounting Standards No. 115 (SFAS No. 115), "Accounting for Certain Investments in Debt and Equity Securities." The Company's policy is to hold all investments in securities until they mature. Accordingly, the effect of adopting SFAS No. 115 had no impact on the Company's financial position or results of operations. The Company adopted the provisions of SFAS No. 115 at the beginning of fiscal 1993.

. . . .

TRADING SECURITIES OWNED

GENERAL ELECTRIC COMPANY, DECEMBER 31, 1993

Statement of Financial Position

At December 31 (*in millions*)	General Electric Company and Consolidated Affiliates	
	1993	1992
Assets		
. . . .		
GECS trading securities (note 10)	30,165	24,154
Investment securities (note 11)	26,811	11,256

. . . .

Notes to Consolidated Financial Statements

Note 1 — Summary of Significant Accounting Policies

Investment and Trading Securities. On December 31, 1993, the Company adopted Statement of Financial Accounting Standards (SFAS) No. 115, Accounting for Certain Investments in Debt and Equity Securities, which requires that investments in debt securities and marketable equity securities be designated as trading, held-to-maturity or available-for-sale. Trading securities are reported at fair value, with changes in fair value included in earnings. Investment securities include both available-for-sale and held-to-maturity securities. Available-for-sale securities are reported at fair value, with net unrealized gains and losses that would be available to share owners included in equity. Held-to-maturity debt securities are reported at amortized cost. See notes 10 and 11 for a discussion of the classification and reporting of these securities at December 31, 1992. For all investment securities, unrealized losses that are other than temporary are recognized in earnings.

. . . .

Note 10

GECS Trading Securities

December 31 (*in millions*)	1993	1992
U.S. Government and federal agency securities	$19,543	$16,172
Corporate stocks, bonds and non-U.S. securities	8,969	5,960
Mortgage loans	1,292	974
State and municipal securities	361	1,048
	$30,165	$24,154

The balance of GECS' trading securities at December 31, 1992, included investments in equity securities held by insurance affiliates at a fair value of $1,505 million, with unrealized pretax gains of $94 million (net of unrealized pretax losses of $37 million) included in equity. At December 31, 1993, equity securities held by insurance affiliates were classified as investment securities (see note 11).

A significant portion of GECS' trading securities at December 31, 1993, was pledged as collateral for bank loans and repurchase agreements in connection with securities broker-dealer operations.

Note 11 — Investment Securities

GE's investment securities were classified as available-for-sale at year-end 1993 and 1992. Carrying value was substantially the same as fair value at both year ends.

At December 31, 1993, GECS' investment securities were classified as available-for-sale and reported at fair value, including net unrealized gains of $1,261 million before taxes. At December 31, 1992, investment securities of $9,033 million were classified as available-for-sale and were reported at the lower of aggregate amortized cost or fair value. The balance of the 1992 investment securities portfolio was carried at amortized cost.

A summary of GECS' investment securities follows.

GECS Investment Securities

(*in millions*)	Amortized Cost	Estimated Fair Value	Gross Unrealized Gains (a)	Gross Unrealized Losses (a)
December 31, 1993				
Corporate, non-U.S. and other	$11,448	$11,595	$ 206	$ (59)
State and municipal	8,859	9,636	786	(9)
Mortgage-backed	2,487	2,507	31	(11)
Equity	1,517	1,826	393	(84)
U.S. government and federal agency	1,220	1,228	15	(7)
	$25,531	$26,792	$1,431	$(170)
December 31, 1992				
Corporate, non-U.S. and other	$ 4,097	$ 4,167	$ 70	$ —
State and municipal	6,626	6,951	339	(14)
Mortgage-backed	246	252	7	(1)
U.S. government and federal agency	255	264	10	(1)
	$11,224	$11,634	$ 426	$ (16)

(a)   December 31, 1992 amounts include gross unrealized gains and losses of $32 million and $5 million, respectively, on investment securities carried at amortized cost.

Contractual maturities of debt securities, other than mortgage-backed securities, at December 31, 1993, are shown below.

GECS Contractual Maturities (excluding mortgage-backed securities)

(*in millions*)	Amortized Cost	Estimated Fair Value
Due in		
1994	$2,665	$2,696
1995–1998	4,326	4,476
1999–2003	4,316	4,429
2004 and later	10,220	10,858

It is expected that actual maturities will differ from contractual maturities because borrowers have the right to call or prepay certain obligations, sometimes without call or prepayment penalties. Proceeds from sales of investment securities in 1993 were $6,112 million ($3,514 million in 1992 and $2,814 million in 1991). Gross realized gains were $173 million in 1993 ($171 million in 1992 and $106 million in 1991). Gross realized losses were $34 million in 1993 ($4 million in 1992 and $9 million in 1991).

INTERNATIONAL ALUMINUM CORP., JUNE 30, 1994

Consolidated Balance Sheets
June 30, 1994 and 1993

	1994	1993
Assets		
Current assets:		
. . . .		
Short-term investments	9,727,000	14,407,000
. . . .		

Notes to Consolidated Financial Statements

Note 1. Significant Accounting Policies and Procedures

. . . .

(b) Short-Term Investments

Short-term investments include preferred stocks, certificates of deposit and money market funds.

During fiscal year 1993, the Company adopted Statement of Financial Accounting Standards No. 115 — Accounting for Certain Investments in Debt and Equity Securities. The preferred stocks are classified as "Trading Securities"; consequently, unrealized holding gains/losses are being currently recognized. Investment income includes unrealized holding losses of $581,000 in 1994 and unrealized holding gains of $487,000 in 1993.

. . . .

INTERNATIONAL THOROUGHBRED BREEDERS INC., JUNE 30, 1994

International Thoroughbred Breeders, Inc. and Subsidiaries
Consolidated Balance Sheets
As of June 30, 1994 and 1993

	June 30,	
	1994	1993
Assets		
Current Assets:		
Cash	$2,683,361	$1,744,475
Short-Term Investments	13,392,730	13,593,180
Total Cash and Cash Equivalents	16,076,091	15,337,655
Restricted Cash and Trading Investments	2,690,072	1,945,017
. . . .		

International Thoroughbred Breeders, Inc. and Subsidiaries
Notes to Financial Statements
For the Years Ended June 30, 1994, 1993, and 1992

(2) Investments

Short-term investments, classified as cash equivalents, consist of interest-bearing certificates of deposit, repurchase agreements and commercial paper, whose cost approximates fair value.

Other investments consist of trading securities whose carrying amount is a reasonable estimate of fair value. Fair value is determined by reference to quoted market prices. There was no unrealized gain or loss on trading securities as of June 30, 1994, as cost approximates fair value. The basis on which cost was determined in computing realized gains or losses on trading securities was the specific identification method.

(18) New Authoritative Pronouncements

Statement of Financial Accounting Standards (SFAS) No. 115, "Accounting for Certain Investments in Debt and Equity Securities," is effective for fiscal years beginning after December 15, 1993. The Company adopted SFAS 115 on June 30, 1994. (See Note 2.) The adoption of SFAS No. 115 did not have a material effect on the financial statements.

ISRAMCO INC., DECEMBER 31, 1993

Isramco Inc. and Subsidiaries
Consolidated Balance Sheets
December 31, 1993 and 1992
(in thousands except for share information)

	1993	1992
Assets		
Current Assets:		
. . . .		
Marketable Securities, at Market (Notes 1 and 7)	4,452	1,645
. . . .		

Isramco Inc. and Subsidiaries
Consolidated Statements of Operations
(in thousands except for share information)

	Year Ended December 31, 1993	Year Ended December 31, 1992	Nine Months Ended December 31, 1991
Revenues:			
. . . .			
Gain on Marketable Securities (Notes 1 and 7)	2,581	22	95
. . . .			

Isramco Inc. and Subsidiaries
Notes to Consolidated Financial Statements

Note 1 — Summary of Significant Accounting Policies

. . . .

(d) Marketable Securities

During the year ended December 31, 1993, the Company adopted SFAS 115, "Accounting for Certain Investments in Debt and Equity Securities." SFAS 115 requires that marketable securities held for trading be recorded at their market value. Company management considers the Company's marketable securities to be held for trading. Similarly, Company management considers that the Isramco-Negev 2 Limited Partnership units held by the Company are held for trading. There was no cumulative effect from the change since marketable securities were written down to their market value at December 31, 1992, because cost exceeded market value. SFAS 115 also requires purchases and sales of marketable securities held for trading to be classified as cash flows from operating activities. The financial statements for the year ended December 31, 1992, and the nine months ended December 31, 1991, have not been restated to reflect such change in classification.

Included in marketable securities is an investment in Isramco-Negev 2 Limited Partnership units (see Note 2). On September 30, 1992, the Company purchased warrants to subscribe to an additional 8,875,969 partnership units and subscribed to such units for an aggregate cost of approximately $796,000. The warrants which had an expiration date of September 30, 1992 were, and the partnership units are, traded on the Tel-Aviv Stock Exchange. The market value per unit was $0.09 and $0.06 at December 31, 1993 and 1992, respectively. The Company entered into an agreement with a third party to effectuate the sale of these units in the sole discretion of and in amounts determined by the third party acting as a trustee, provided that the price at which sales would be affected would not be less than the amount set forth in the agreement. At December 31, 1993, the Company owned less than 1% of the total limited partnership units outstanding.

. . . .

Sale of marketable securities resulted in realized gains of $825,465, $38,738, and $95,137 for the years ended December 31, 1993 and 1992, and the nine months ended December 31, 1991. The first-in, first-out method is used for the cost of securities to determine the gain or loss on a sale.

At December 31, 1992, the Company had unrealized gains of $177,090 and unrealized losses of $193,487. The net unrealized loss on marketable securities of $16,397 was included in gain on marketable securities. At December 31, 1993, the Company had net unrealized gains of $1,738,667 on securities held for trading. The change in net unrealized holding gain of $1,755,064 is included in gain on marketable securities.

Marketable securities consist of the following:

	December 31, 1993		December 31, 1992	
	Cost	Market Value	Cost	Market Value
Debentures	$ 101,101	$ 101,438	$ 7,593	$ 8,266
Convertible Debentures	92,934	106,295	2,597	2,578
Investment Trust Fund	1,424,827	1,730,564	581,209	710,122
Warrants/Options	0	14,952	9,140	22,631
Shares (1)	1,094,351	2,498,631	1,061,735	902,280
	$2,713,213	$4,451,880	$1,662,274	$1,645,877

(1) Includes cost and market value of Isramco-Negev 2 Limited Partnership units of $20,043 and $45,978, and $797,898 and $614,812, at December 31, 1993 and 1992, respectively.

. . . .

Note 7 — Subsequent Events

As of March 25, 1994, the market value of securities held for trading owned at December 31, 1993 was approximately $950,000 less than the market value at December 31, 1993.

MINNESOTA POWER, DECEMBER 31, 1993

Minnesota Power
Consolidated Balance Sheet

December 31	1993	1992
	(*in thousands*)	
. . . .		
Investment and Other Assets		
Securities and other investments	123,511	200,509
. . . .		
Current Assets		
. . . .		
Trading securities	98,244	—
. . . .		
Capitalization (Page 32)		
. . . .		
Net unrealized gain on securities investments	1,488	—

Consolidated Statement of Income
For the Year Ended December 31

	1993	1992	1991
	(*in thousands except per share amounts*)		
. . . .			
Other Income and (Deductions)			
Securities investment and interest income	25,637	39,342	35,922
Income from equity investments	4,729	4,352	12,791
. . . .			

Notes to Consolidated Financial Statements

1 — Summary of Significant Accounting Policies

. . . .

Securities Investments. Effective December 31, 1993, the Company adopted Statement of Financial Accounting Standards No. 115, "Accounting for Certain Investments in Debt and Equity Securities" (SFAS 115). As a result of adopting SFAS 115, the Company's securities investments that are bought and held principally for the purpose of selling them in the near term are classified as trading securities. Trading securities are recorded at fair value on the balance sheet in current assets with the change in fair value during the period included in earnings. Securities investments that the Company has the positive intent and ability to hold to maturity are classified as held-to-maturity securities and recorded at amortized cost in investments and other assets. Securities investments not classified as either held-to-maturity or trading securities are classified as available-for-sale securities. Available-for-sale securities are recorded at fair value in investments and other assets on the balance sheet with the change in fair value during the period recorded as a separate component of common stock equity. If the fair value of any of the available-for-sale or held-to-maturity securities declines below cost and the decline is considered to be other than temporary, the securities are written down to fair value and the losses are charged to earnings. Realized gains and losses are computed on each specific investment sold. Prior to December 31, 1993, the Company carried securities investments at cost. (See note 8.)

. . . .

8 — Securities Investments

The majority of the Company's securities investments are investment-grade stocks of other utility companies and are considered by the Company to be conservative investments.

The Company sells common stock securities short and enters into bond futures contracts as part of an overall investment portfolio hedge strategy. Selling common stock securities short and entering bond futures contracts create potential off-balance-sheet market risk to the Company. At December 31, 1993, the Company had approximately $76.1 million of short stock sales outstanding and $29.4 million of bond futures contracts.

The Company adopted SFAS 115 on December 31, 1993. SFAS 115 established standards of financial accounting and reporting for investments in equity securities that have readily determinable fair values and for all investments in debt securities. Those investments are classified and accounted for in three categories. The Company's securities investments that are bought and held principally for the purpose of selling them in the near term are classified as trading securities. Trading securities are recorded at fair value on the balance sheet in current assets, with the change in fair value during the period included in earnings. Securities investments that the Company has the positive intent and ability to hold to maturity are classified as held-to-maturity securities and recorded at amortized cost in investments and other assets. Securities investments not classified as either held-to-maturity or trading securities are classified as available-for-sale securities. Available-for-sale securities are recorded at fair value in investments and other assets on the balance sheet, with the change in fair value during the period excluded from earnings and recorded net of tax as a separate component of common stock equity. If the fair value of any of the available-for-sale or held-to-maturity securities declines below cost and the decline is considered to be other than temporary, the securities are written down to fair value and the losses are charged to earnings. The impact on 1993 earnings of adopting SFAS 115 included recognition of a $ 1 million pretax loss for the net unrealized losses on the Company's trading securities. The fair value (carrying value) of the Company's securities investments is as follows:

| | December 31, 1993 (in thousands) | | | |
	Cost	Gross Unrealized Gain	(Loss)	Fair Value
Trading securities				$ 98,244
Available-for-sale securities				
Common stock	$ 11,267	$ 306	$(463)	$ 11,110
Preferred stock	91,191	3,101	(407)	93,885
	$102,458	$3,407	$(870)	$104,995
Held-to-maturity securities				
Leveraged preferred stock	$ 7,179			7,179
Total securities investments				112,174
Other investments	$11,337			11,337
Total securities and other investments				$123,511

At Dec. 31, 1992, the aggregate carrying value of the Company's securities investments totaled $200.5 million and was comprised of the following types of securities; preferred stock, $110.4 million; common stock, $77.5 million; and other, $12.6 million. The market value of these securities investments was not significantly different from the cost (carrying value of these investments).

NL INDUSTRIES INC., DECEMBER 31, 1993

NL Industries, Inc. and Subsidiaries
Consolidated Balance Sheets
December 31, 1992 and 1993
(in thousands, except per share data)

	1992	1993
. . . .		
Other assets:		
Marketable securities	23,581	18,428
. . . .		
Shareholders' deficit:		
. . . .		
Adjustments:		
. . . .		
Marketable securities	(896)	(2,164)

. . . .

NL Industries, Inc. and Subsidiaries
Consolidated Statements of Operations
Years Ended December 31, 1991, 1992, and 1993
(in thousands, except per share data)

	1991	1992	1993
. . . .			
Revenues and other income:			
. . . .			
Securities transactions	(53,092)	(6,018)	4,363
. . . .			
Loss before extraordinary items and cumulative effect of changes in accounting principles	(23,985)	(44,596)	(83,211)
. . . .			
Cumulative effect of changes in accounting principles	—	(31,804)	1,217
Net loss	$(16,462)	$(76,400)	$(109,809)

. . . .

NL Industries, Inc. and Subsidiaries
Consolidated Statements of Shareholders' Deficit
Years Ended December 31, 1991, 1992, and 1993
(in thousands, except per share data)

	Marketable Securities
Balance at December 31, 1992	(896)
Adjustments	(51)
Cumulative effect of change in accounting principle	(1,217)
Balance at December 31, 1993	$(2,164)

NL Industries, Inc. and Subsidiaries
Notes to Consolidated Financial Statements

Note 2 — Summary of Significant Accounting Policies

. . . .

Marketable Securities and Securities Transactions. The Company adopted Statement of Financial Accounting Standards ("SFAS") No. 115, "Accounting for Certain Investments in Debt and Equity Securities," effective December 31, 1993, and the Company's marketable securities were classified as either "available-for-sale" or "trading" and are carried at market. Unrealized gains and losses on trading securities are recognized in income currently. Unrealized gains and losses on available-for-sale securities, and the related deferred income tax effects, are accumulated in the marketable securities adjustment component of shareholders' deficit. See Notes 4 and 19.

SFAS No. 115 superseded SFAS No. 12 under which marketable securities were generally carried at the lower of aggregate market or amortized cost and unrealized net gains were not recognized.

Realized gains or losses are computed based on specific identification of the securities sold.

. . . .

Note 4 — Marketable Securities and Securities Transactions

	December 31,	
	1992	1993
	(in thousands)	
Current:		
Marketable equity securities	$ 6,996	$ —
U.S. Treasury securities	93,611	41,045
	$100,607	$41,045
Noncurrent:		
Marketable equity securities	$ 9,192	$ 18,428
U.S. Treasury securities	14,389	—
	$23,581	$18,428
Marketable equity securities:		
Current:		
Unrealized gains	$ 13	$ —
Unrealized losses	(4,233)	—
Cost	11,216	—
Aggregate market	$ 6,996	$ —
Noncurrent:		
Unrealized gains	$ —	$ 33
Unrealized losses	(979)	(2,951)
Cost	10,171	21,346
Aggregate market	$ 9,192	$18,428
Current U.S. Treasury securities:		
Unrealized gains (losses)	$ (59)	$ 52
Cost	93,670	40,993
Aggregate market	$93,611	$41,045

Upon adoption of SFAS No. 115 as of December 31, 1993, the Company classified its portfolio of U.S. Treasury securities as trading securities and its marketable equity securities as available-for-sale.

Net gains and losses from securities transactions are composed of:

	Years Ended December 31,		
	1991	1992	1993
	(in thousands)		
Unrealized gains (losses):			
Marketable equity securities	$ (517)	$ (52)	$2,348
Other securities	2,337	(513)	1,172
Realized gains (losses):			
Marketable equity securities	(52,813)	(528)	(9)
Other securities	4,437	1,006	852
Writedown of noncurrent marketable			
equity securities	(6,536)	(5,931)	—
	$(53,092)	$(6,018)	$4,363

Note 19 — Changes in Accounting Principles

In 1993, the Company adopted SFAS No. 115 (marketable securities) as of December 31, 1993.... The cumulative effect of changes in accounting principles adjustments is shown below.

	Amount Reflected in	
	Earnings	Equity Component
	(in thousands)	
Increase (decrease) in net assets at		
December 31, 1993 — SFAS No. 115:		
Marketable securities	$1,872	$(1,872)
Deferred income taxes	(655)	655
	$1,217	$(1,217)

. . . .

SEALASKA CORPORATION, MARCH 31, 1994

Sealaska Corporation
Consolidated Balance Sheets
(in thousands of dollars)

(Notes 1 and 10)	March 31, 1994	March 31, 1993 (as restated)
Assets		
Current assets:		
Cash	$ 475	$ 503
Investment securities (Note 4)	110,769	90,557

. . . .

Investment securities (Note 4):		
Permanent Fund	72,133	70,979
Endowment Funds	4,319	3,979
Elders' Settlement Trust	4,277	4,070
Other	46,837	46,340
	127,566	125,368

110

Sealaska Corporation
Notes to Consolidated Financial Statements

. . . .

Note 1 — Summary of Significant Accounting Policies

. . . .

Investment Securities. On April 1, 1993, Sealaska adopted Statement of Financial Accounting Standards No. 115 (SFAS 115), Accounting for Certain Investments in Debt and Equity Securities. Under SFAS 115, Sealaska's investment securities (Note 4) are classified as trading securities and are recorded at fair value. Fair value is based upon quoted market prices. Previously, investment securities were stated at the lower of cost or market. The excess of cost over market, relating to marketable securities included in Sealaska's investment portfolio, was included in the determination of earnings. Gain or loss on the sale of marketable securities is determined on a specific identification basis.

Sealaska has designated certain investments for long-term uses, and therefore classifies these amounts as non-current.

. . . .

Note 4 — Investment Securities

Investment securities consist of the following:

(in thousands of dollars)	March 31, 1994 Carrying and Fair Value Amount	March 31, 1993 Carrying Amount	Fair Value
Domestic			
Money market funds	$106,985	$ 14,031	$ 14,031
Certificates of deposit	4,140	12,211	12,211
Commercial paper	536	2,200	2,185
Govt. bonds & notes	71,021	97,728	97,820
Corporate bonds & notes	20,759	38,832	39,332
Common stock	6,902	40,317	40,515
Mutual funds		8,863	8,963
Other	2,100	1,743	1,743
International			
Cash & cash equivalents	7,099		
Debt securities	9,506		
Equity securities	9,287		
Total	238,335	215,925	$216,700
Less: current portion	(110,769)	(90,557)	
Noncurrent investment securities	$127,566	$125,368	

In a September 19, 1987 advisory vote, the majority of shareholders voted to establish a Permanent Fund with no less than 50 percent of the NOL sales proceeds. Accordingly, the Sealaska board of directors has designated certain amounts arising from net operating loss (NOL) transactions (Note 10) and related investment earnings for long-term uses (Permanent Fund) and, accordingly, they are not available for current operations.

Additionally, endowments have been established for which the earnings accrue to the benefit of the Sealaska Heritage Foundation scholarship program and the Alaska Native Brotherhood. Further, investment securities relating to deferred NOL income (Note 10) are classified as noncurrent assets.

. . . .

During the years ended March 31, 1994 and 1993, Sealaska realized net gains of $1,190,000 and $3,000,000, respectively, on the sales of securities, including gains and losses on futures contracts. Financial markets declined significantly in the last quarter of fiscal year 1994. Sealaska had unrealized net gains (losses) of ($3,785,000) and $775,000 at March 31, 1994 and 1993, respectively, which included losses on open futures contracts.